America Loves
SOUPS & STEWS

From stocks to noodles to dumplings to crackers and croutons ... hot soups and cold soups; long-simmering soups and stews; and quick soups; meal-mate soups; fish and seafood, meat and poultry and vegetable whole-meal soups and stews ... This is the book of satisfying soups and stews ... the book that welcomes you to the truly special flavor and aroma of a delicious, homemade soup or stew.

Better Homes and Gardens®
SOUPS & STEWS COOK BOOK

Better Homes and Gardens®

SOUPS & STEWS COOK BOOK

GOLDEN APPLE PUBLISHERS

THE BETTER HOMES AND GARDENS[R] SOUPS & STEWS COOK BOOK
*A Golden Apple Publication / published by arrangement with
Meredith Corporation*

PRINTING HISTORY

Golden Apple edition / June 1985

Golden Apple is a trademark of Golden Apple Publishers

ISBN 0-553-19840-8

PRINTED IN THE UNITED STATES OF AMERICA

H   0 9 8 7 6 5 4 3 2 1

CONTENTS

SATISFYING SOUPS AND STEWS

The truly special flavor and aroma of a homemade soup or stew is always welcome. Whether you choose a delicate broth or a thick and meaty bean soup, a spectacular wine and seafood stew or a nourishing vegetable soup, it's an eating experience you'll enjoy.

Prepare a soup or stew for any part of the meal. In Meal-Mate Soups, you'll find first-course soups, and soups that turn a sandwich or salad into a meal. Some sweet cold soups even double as dessert or a treat for breakfast or brunch. And any of these can make a lively snack—a cold one when the temperature rises, or a hot one for a chilly day.

If you're looking for a main dish, leaf through Whole-Meal Soups and Stews. These stand alone; complete the meal with a salad and bread or crackers.

The last section of the book is a guide to Soup-Making Basics. Here you'll learn how easy it is to make a long-simmering stock from scratch. Also included are recipes for noodles, dumplings, crackers, and croutons —the extras that make your homemade soups and stews special.

Of course, you needn't spend all day in the kitchen to make a satisfying soup. Commercial products combine with fresh ingredients to make delicious soups in a hurry. Such recipes are grouped on the pages labeled Quick Soups. They're perfect for busy cooks.

A soup or stew is a lot more than a side dish to eat with a sandwich. Whether you're preparing an appetizer or a dessert, a special dinner for company or a quick lunch for the kids, you'll find all the soups and stews you need in this book.

MEAL-MATE SOUPS

Hot & Cold Soups

When you need a soup to complete a meal, choose from those in this chapter. Sample clear broths, creamy chowders, and chilly soups for appetizers that fit a variety of menus and serving styles—from very casual to very elegant.

A steaming bowl of soup, particularly one with vegetables or meat and vegetables, completes a sandwich or main-dish salad meal.

Serve cold soups according to their character. All are appropriate as first courses or snacks, and cold fruit soups can be intriguing desserts, as well.

HOT SOUPS

Summer Vegetable-Chicken Soup

If desired, slice the broccoli while the chicken cooks—

8 ounces broccoli
1 whole chicken
   breast, split
¾ cup water
1 medium onion,
   chopped (½ cup)
1 stalk celery, thinly
   sliced (½ cup)
3 cups chicken broth
   (see tip, page 174)

1 teaspoon lemon
   juice
¼ teaspoon dried
   thyme, crushed
⅛ teaspoon pepper
3 small tomatoes,
   peeled and cut
   into thin wedges

Remove the broccoli buds; thinly slice stalks (you should have a total of 2 cups buds and stalks). Set aside. In medium saucepan combine chicken, water, onion, and celery. Bring to boiling. Reduce heat; cover and simmer for 15 to 20 minutes or till chicken is tender. Remove chicken; cool slightly. Discard skin and bones; cut meat into short strips. Return chicken to cooking liquid.

Stir broccoli buds and stalks, chicken broth, lemon juice, thyme, and pepper into cooking liquid. Bring to boiling. Reduce heat; cover and simmer for 3 minutes. Add tomatoes; simmer, covered, about 4 minutes or till broccoli is crisp-tender and tomatoes are heated through. Season to taste with salt and pepper. Makes 4 to 6 servings.

Microwave cooking directions: Remove the broccoli buds; thinly slice stalks. In 2-quart nonmetal casserole combine chicken, water, onion, celery, and broccoli buds and stalks. Cook, covered with waxed paper, in countertop microwave oven on high power about 12 minutes or till chicken is tender. Remove chicken; cool slightly. Discard skin and bones; cut meat into short strips. Return chicken to casserole.

Stir in chicken broth, lemon juice, thyme, and pepper. Micro-cook, covered, for 3 to 4 minutes. Add tomatoes. Micro-cook, uncovered, about 45 seconds or till broccoli is crisp-tender and tomatoes are heated through. Season to taste.

Pea-Cottage Cheese Soup

1 medium potato, chopped (1 cup)	¼ teaspoon salt
2 stalks celery, chopped (1 cup)	⅛ teaspoon pepper
1 medium onion, chopped (½ cup)	2 cups cream-style cottage cheese
½ cup chicken broth (see tip, page 174)	1 8-ounce can peas, drained
½ teaspoon dried basil, crushed	1 cup milk

In 2-quart saucepan combine potato, celery, onion, chicken broth, basil, salt, and pepper. Bring to boiling. Reduce heat; cover and simmer for 15 minutes or till vegetables are tender.

Meanwhile, in blender container combine cottage cheese, peas, and milk; cover and blend till smooth. Stir into vegetables in saucepan; heat through. Makes 6 servings.

Chickumber Chowder

1 medium onion,
   chopped (½ cup)
¼ cup butter *or*
   margarine
¼ cup all-purpose
   flour
½ teaspoon seasoned
   salt
¼ teaspoon white
   pepper
3 cups chicken broth
   (see tip, page 174)
5 medium cucumbers
   (about 2½
   pounds), peeled,

halved length-
   wise, seeded, and
   cut up
• • •
2 cups cubed cooked
   chicken *or* turkey
   (12 ounces)
½ cup long grain rice
2 tablespoons lemon
   juice
2 bay leaves
• • •
1 cup light cream
¼ cup snipped parsley

In 3-quart saucepan cook onion in butter or margarine till tender but not brown. Blend in flour, seasoned salt, and white pepper. Stir in chicken broth. Cook and stir till thickened and bubbly. Add cucumber. Cover and simmer for 10 minutes. Pour *half* the mixture at a time into blender container. Cover and blend on medium speed for 30 seconds. Return all to saucepan.

Stir in chicken or turkey, uncooked rice, lemon juice, and bay leaves. Return to boiling. Reduce heat; cover and simmer 20 to 25 minutes or till rice is tender. Remove bay leaves. Stir in cream and parsley; heat through. Season to taste with salt and pepper. Garnish with snipped parsley, if desired. Makes 6 servings.

Chinese Squash Soup

If you can't find Chinese squash at your supermarket or Oriental food store, substitute chayote, Chinese melon, or vegetable marrow—

¼ cup chopped onion
½ teaspoon curry powder
2 tablespoons cooking oil
2 tablespoons all-purpose flour
4 cups chicken broth (see tip, page 174)
2 tomatoes, peeled and chopped
1 apple, peeled and chopped
½ cup chopped carrot
¼ cup chopped green pepper

2 tablespoons snipped parsley
1 tablespoon lemon juice
1 teaspoon sugar
¼ teaspoon salt
Dash pepper
1 Chinese squash, peeled and chopped (1½ cups)
1 cup diced cooked chicken

In 3-quart saucepan cook chopped onion and curry powder in hot oil till onion is tender but not brown. Blend in the flour. Stir in chicken broth, chopped tomatoes, apple, carrot, green pepper, parsley, lemon juice, sugar, salt, and pepper. Bring mixture to boiling, stirring occasionally. Reduce heat; cover and simmer for 15 minutes. Stir in Chinese squash and cooked chicken; simmer 15 minutes more or till squash is tender. Makes 6 to 8 servings.

Turkey Soup with Danish Dumplings

A good use for turkey bones that have some meat left on them—

1 meaty turkey
  carcass
8 cups water
1 tablespoon instant
  chicken bouillon
  granules
  • • •
1 16-ounce can toma-
  toes, cut up
2 stalks celery, sliced
  (1 cup)
1 medium turnip,
  peeled and diced
  (1 cup)

1 medium carrot,
  sliced (½ cup)
1 medium onion,
  chopped
  (½ cup)
¼ cup snipped parsley
1 to 2 teaspoons salt
1 bay leaf
  Danish Dumplings
  (see recipe, page
  179)

Cut up the turkey carcass to fit into a large Dutch oven. In the Dutch oven combine the carcass, water, and chicken bouillon granules. Bring to boiling. Reduce heat; cover and simmer for 1½ hours. Remove turkey carcass.

When carcass is cool enough to handle, remove meat from bones; discard bones. Return meat to cooking liquid along with *undrained* tomatoes, celery, turnip, carrot, onion, parsley, salt, and bay leaf. Bring to boiling. Reduce heat; cover and simmer 30 minutes or till vegetables are nearly tender. Remove bay leaf.

Drop Danish Dumpling dough from a tablespoon to make 12 mounds atop bubbling soup. Cover and simmer 20 minutes (do not lift cover). Makes 6 servings.

Pumpkin Soup

1 pound meaty beef short ribs
4 cups water

• • •

8 ounces pumpkin *or* winter squash, peeled, cubed,
    and cut up (about 3 cups)
1 medium potato, peeled and quartered
1 large carrot, quartered
1 medium onion, quartered
1½ teaspoons salt
¼ teaspoon white pepper

• • •

½ cup light cream (optional)

In 4-quart Dutch oven or large saucepan brown short
ribs over low heat (add some cooking oil, if needed).
Add water. Bring to boiling. Reduce heat; cover and
simmer 1 hour. Remove ribs from broth. When ribs
are cool enough to handle, cut meat from bones and
return meat to broth; discard bones.

Add pumpkin or squash, potato, carrot, onion, salt,
and white pepper to broth. Cover and simmer over
medium heat for 45 minutes.

Pour *half* the mixture into blender container (or
one-third of the mixture into food processor); cover
and blend till smooth. Return blended mixture to
saucepan. Repeat with remaining mixture. Heat
through. Pour soup into individual soup bowls. Top
each serving with a little cream, if desired. Do not stir
before serving. Makes 6 servings.

Creamy Potato Soup

A potato soup with pieces of carrot and celery and the tang of dairy sour cream—

4 slices bacon, cut up
3 medium potatoes, peeled and chopped (3 cups)
1 large onion, chopped (1 cup)
1 medium carrot, chopped (½ cup)
1 stalk celery, chopped (½ cup)

4 cups milk
2 teaspoons salt
¼ teaspoon pepper
• • •
1 cup dairy sour cream
2 tablespoons all-purpose flour
2 teaspoons paprika

In large saucepan cook bacon till crisp. Drain bacon, reserving 3 tablespoons drippings in pan. Set bacon aside. Add chopped potatoes, onion, carrot, and celery to bacon drippings. Cover and cook over low heat about 20 minutes or till potatoes are tender, stirring occasionally. Stir in the milk, salt, and pepper; bring mixture to boiling.

Stir together sour cream, flour, and paprika; gradually stir about *1 cup* of the hot mixture into sour cream mixture. Return to remaining hot mixture in saucepan. Cook and stir just till mixture bubbles. Top with the bacon pieces. Serve immediately. Makes 6 to 8 servings.

Squash and Pea Soup

1 cup dry split peas
3 slices bacon, cut up
1 cup chopped onion
1 cup chopped green pepper
1 teaspoon instant chicken bouillon granules
1 12-ounce package frozen mashed squash
1 cup light cream

Rinse peas; set aside. In large saucepan cook bacon till crisp; drain, reserving drippings in pan. Set bacon aside. Cook onion and green pepper in drippings just till tender; add peas, bouillon granules, 4 cups *water*, ¾ teaspoon *salt*, and ⅛ teaspoon *pepper*. Bring to boiling. Reduce heat; cover and simmer 1½ hours. Stir in frozen squash; cover and simmer 20 minutes or till heated through. Stir in cream and bacon; heat through. Makes 4 servings.

Easy Vegetable Soup

4 cups beef broth
  (see tip, page 174)
1 16-ounce can
  garbanzo beans,
  drained
1 16-ounce can
  tomatoes, cut up
1 8-ounce can cut
  green beans,
  drained
½ cup shell macaroni
½ cup chopped onion
½ cup finely chopped
  carrot
½ teaspoon dried
  basil, crushed
¼ teaspoon dried rose-
  mary, crushed
¼ teaspoon dried
  thyme, crushed

In 4-quart Dutch oven combine all ingredients. Cover and simmer 30 to 40 minutes or till vegetables are tender. Makes 8 servings.

Buttermilk-Corn Chowder

2 slices bacon, cut up
1 small onion,
    chopped (¼ cup)
2 medium potatoes,
    peeled and cubed
    (2 cups)
2 cups fresh whole
    kernel corn *or*
    1 10-ounce pack-
    age frozen whole
    kernel corn
2 cups chicken broth
    (see tip, page 174)

1 stalk celery,
    chopped (½ cup)
½ teaspoon salt
¼ teaspoon pepper
• • •
2 tablespoons all-
    purpose flour
2 cups buttermilk
    Paprika *or* snipped
    parsley (optional)

In a 3-quart saucepan cook bacon till crisp. Drain bacon, reserving drippings in pan. Set bacon aside. Cook the chopped onion in bacon drippings till tender but not brown. Add the potatoes, corn, *1½ cups* of the chicken broth, the celery, salt, and pepper. Bring to boiling. Reduce heat; cover and simmer for 15 to 20 minutes or till vegetables are tender.

Combine flour and remaining ½ cup chicken broth; add to vegetable mixture. Cook and stir till thickened and bubbly. Reduce heat to low. Stir in buttermilk; heat through but *do not boil*. Top each serving with some of the bacon. Garnish with paprika or snipped parsley, if desired. Serve immediately. Makes 6 servings.

Chinese Hot Sour Soup

Make green onion fans by slicing the onion tops length-wise, taking care to leave greens attached at the top of the onion bulb. Chill in a bowl of ice water until the tops curl—

4 ounces lean bone-less pork
1 tablespoon cooking oil
4 cups chicken broth (see tip, page 174)
1 8-ounce can bamboo shoots, drained
1 3-ounce can sliced mushrooms, drained
2 tablespoons vinegar

1 tablespoon soy sauce
¼ teaspoon salt
¼ teaspoon white pepper *or* pepper
1 tablespoon corn-starch
2 tablespoons cold water
1 well-beaten egg
Green onion fans

Partially freeze meat for easier slicing. Slice pork thinly into bite-size pieces. In 3-quart saucepan cook pork pieces in hot oil till lightly browned. Drain and set aside.

In same saucepan bring chicken broth to boiling. Add pork, bamboo shoots, and mushrooms. Simmer 5 minutes. Add vinegar, soy sauce, salt, and pepper. Blend together the cornstarch and water; stir into soup. Cook and stir till slightly thickened and bubbly. Stir broth to swirl; pour the beaten egg into center of swirl. Cook and stir 1 to 2 minutes more. Garnish each serving with a green onion fan. Makes 5 servings.

Herbed Tomato-Vegetable Soup

Prepare this soup with either canned or fresh tomatoes—

1 medium onion,
chopped (½ cup)
2 tablespoons butter
or margarine

• • •

4 cups water
1 28-ounce can tomatoes, cut up *or*
2½ pounds fresh
tomatoes, peeled
and chopped
(4 cups)
2 medium carrots,
thinly sliced
(1 cup)
2 stalks celery,
chopped (1 cup)

1 tablespoon instant
chicken bouillon
granules
1 teaspoon sugar
1 teaspoon dried
basil, crushed
½ teaspoon salt
½ teaspoon dried
thyme, crushed
¼ teaspoon dried
savory, crushed
⅛ teaspoon ground
mace
⅛ teaspoon pepper
Few dashes bottled
hot pepper sauce

In large saucepan cook onion in butter or margarine till tender but not brown. Stir in water, *undrained* tomatoes, carrots, celery, bouillon granules, sugar, basil, salt, thyme, savory, mace, pepper, and hot pepper sauce. Bring to boiling. Reduce heat; cover and simmer about 40 minutes or till vegetables are tender. Makes 8 servings.

Vegetable Soup with Green Noodles

1 medium rutabaga,
    diced (4 cups)
2 large onions,
    chopped (2 cups)
2 stalks celery, sliced
    (1 cup)
2 medium carrots,
    sliced (1 cup)
1 medium green
    pepper, chopped
    (½ cup)
1 clove garlic, minced
¼ cup butter *or*
    margarine

5 cups water
1 16-ounce can
    tomatoes, cut up
1 tablespoon snipped
    parsley
1 tablespoon salt
1 teaspoon sugar
½ teaspoon dried
    dillweed
¼ teaspoon pepper
    Green Noodles (see
    recipe, page 178)

In 5-quart Dutch oven combine the rutabaga, onions, celery, carrots, green pepper, garlic, and butter or margarine. Cover and cook about 10 minutes or till onion is tender but not brown, stirring occasionally.

Stir in the water, *undrained* tomatoes, parsley, salt, sugar, dried dillweed, and pepper. Bring to boiling. Reduce heat; cover and simmer 40 minutes. Stir in Green Noodles; cook, uncovered, for 10 to 12 minutes or till noodles are tender. Makes 8 to 10 servings.

Wonton Soup

1 beaten egg
¼ cup finely chopped onion
¼ cup finely chopped water chestnuts
1 tablespoon soy sauce
2 teaspoons grated fresh gingerroot
½ teaspoon sugar
¼ teaspoon salt
⅛ teaspoon pepper
½ pound ground pork
1 4½-ounce can shrimp, drained, deveined, and chopped
40 wonton skins or 10 egg roll skins, cut into quarters

8 cups water
• • •
6 cups chicken broth (see tip, page 174)
1 cup coarsely shredded Chinese cabbage
1 cup thinly sliced fresh mushrooms
1 6-ounce package frozen pea pods, thawed and halved lengthwise
½ cup thinly sliced bamboo shoots
4 green onions, bias-sliced into 1½-inch lengths

For filling, in bowl combine egg, onion, water chestnuts, soy sauce, gingerroot, sugar, salt, and pepper. Add ground pork and chopped shrimp; mix well.

Position wonton skin with one point toward you (refer to tip on page 72). Spoon 1 rounded teaspoon of filling just below center of skin. Fold bottom point of wonton skin over the filling; tuck point under filling. Roll up skin and filling, leaving about 1 inch at the top of skin. Moisten the right-hand corner of skin with water. Grasp the two lower corners of triangle; bring these corners toward you below the filling. Overlap the left-hand corner over the right-hand corner; press to seal. Use 20 for soup; wrap, label, and freeze remaining 20 filled wontons.

In a large saucepan bring 8 cups *water* to boiling. Drop the wontons, one at a time, into boiling water. Simmer, uncovered, about 3 minutes. Remove from heat and rinse with cold water; drain well.

In same large saucepan bring chicken broth to boiling. Add Chinese cabbage, mushrooms, pea pods, bamboo shoots, and the precooked wontons. Simmer, uncovered, 4 to 5 minutes. Stir in green onion. Ladle soup into individual serving bowls. Makes 6 to 8 servings.

Creole Tomato Soup

¼ cup sliced green onion	¼ cup long grain rice
1 clove garlic, minced	1 teaspoon sugar
1 tablespoon butter *or* margarine	½ teaspoon salt
	¼ teaspoon dried thyme, crushed
2 12-ounce cans (3 cups) vegetable juice cocktail	1 bay leaf
	1 4½-ounce can shrimp, drained and deveined
1 cup water	

In saucepan cook onion and garlic in butter or margarine till tender but not brown. Add vegetable juice cocktail, water, uncooked rice, sugar, salt, thyme, and bay leaf. Bring to boiling. Reduce heat; cover and simmer about 25 minutes or till rice is tender. Stir in shrimp. Heat through. Remove bay leaf before serving. Makes 4 servings.

Shrimp-Vegetable Broth

Float avocado slices atop servings of this soup—

3 cups water
2 medium carrots,
    thinly sliced
    (1 cup)
4 teaspoons instant
    chicken bouillon
    granules

• • •

4 ounces frozen
    shelled shrimp
    (about 1 cup)

½ cup thinly sliced
    fresh mushrooms
½ cup frozen peas
4 green onions, bias-
    sliced into 1-inch
    pieces
1 small avocado,
    seeded, peeled,
    and sliced

In 1½-quart saucepan combine water, carrots, and bouillon granules. Bring to boiling. Reduce heat; cover and simmer for 25 to 30 minutes or till carrots are tender. Add shrimp, mushrooms, and peas. Simmer, uncovered, about 5 minutes or till shrimp and vegetables are tender. Stir in green onions. Ladle into individual serving bowls. Top each serving with avocado slices. Makes 6 to 8 servings.

Microwave cooking directions: Use ingredients as listed above. In 1½-quart nonmetal casserole combine water, carrots, and bouillon granules. Cook, covered, in countertop microwave oven on high power for 12 to 15 minutes or till carrots are tender. Add shrimp, mushrooms, and peas. Micro-cook, covered, for 4 to 5 minutes or till shrimp and vegetables are tender, stirring once. Stir in green onions. Serve as above.

Potato-Tomato Soup

4 cups cubed potatoes
3 medium tomatoes, peeled and chopped (2 cups)
1 cup chopped carrot
1 cup chopped celery

3 10½-ounce cans *condensed* beef broth
1 small bay leaf
2 slices pumpernickel bread
1 cup dairy sour cream

In large saucepan combine potatoes, tomatoes, carrot, celery, beef broth and bay leaf. Bring to boiling. Reduce heat; cover and simmer 20 minutes or till vegetables are tender.

Meanwhile, cube bread; place bread cubes on baking sheet. Toast in 350° oven 10 minutes; set aside. Remove bay leaf from soup. Top each serving with toast cubes and a dollop of sour cream. Makes 8 servings.

Cheese Soup

½ cup finely chopped carrot
½ cup finely chopped onion
¼ cup finely chopped celery
2 tablespoons butter
¼ cup all-purpose flour

1 cup chicken broth (see tip, page 174)
¼ teaspoon salt
2 cups light cream *or* milk
1½ cups shredded American cheese (6 ounces)

In covered saucepan cook carrot, onion, and celery in butter over low heat till tender. Stir in flour. Add broth and salt. Cook and stir till thickened and bubbly. Stir in cream or milk and cheese till cheese melts and soup is heated through. *Do not boil.* Makes 4 to 6 servings.

Creamy Borscht

After the egg yolk–sour cream mixture is added, be sure that the soup does not boil—

4 cups Browned Beef
   Stock (see recipe,
   page 169) *or*
   Vegetable Stock
   (see recipe, page
   175)
4 medium beets,
   peeled and cubed
   (3 cups)
2 medium carrots,
   chopped (1 cup)
1 medium onion,
   chopped (½
   cup)
1 bay leaf

1 tablespoon vinegar
1 teaspoon sugar
1 teaspoon salt
¼ teaspoon pepper
   • • •
½ small head cabbage,
   shredded (3
   cups)
1 16-ounce can
   tomatoes, cut up
2 slightly beaten egg
   yolks
½ cup dairy sour
   cream

In a 4-quart Dutch oven combine Browned Beef Stock or Vegetable Stock, beets, carrots, onion, bay leaf, vinegar, sugar, salt, and pepper. Bring to boiling. Reduce heat; cover and simmer for 40 minutes. Stir in cabbage and *undrained* tomatoes. Cover and cook 30 to 35 minutes more or till vegetables are tender. Remove bay leaf.

Blend egg yolks and sour cream; gradually stir in about *1 cup* of the hot mixture. Return to Dutch oven; heat through, stirring constantly over low heat. *Do not boil*. Serve immediately. Makes 6 to 8 servings.

Green Bean Chowder

1 9-ounce package
   frozen French-
   style green beans
1 cup chopped carrot
1 cup chopped potato
½ cup chopped green
   pepper
1 teaspoon dried
   savory, crushed

¼ teaspoon dried
   dillweed
1 cup dairy sour
   cream
1 tablespoon all-
   purpose flour
2 cups milk

Partially thaw beans; chop and set aside. In 3-quart saucepan mix carrot, potato, green pepper, savory, dillweed, 1 teaspoon *salt*, and ¼ teaspoon *pepper*. Stir in 2 cups *water*. Bring to boiling; reduce heat and simmer 10 minutes. Add beans; cook 5 minutes more or till vegetables are tender. Blend sour cream and flour; stir in about *1 cup* of the hot mixture. Return to saucepan. Stir in milk; heat till slightly thickened; *do not boil*. Makes 8 servings.

Matzo Ball Soup

4 cups chicken broth
   (see tip, page 174)
2 medium carrots,
   sliced

Matzo Balls (see
   recipe, page 181)
2 tablespoons snipped
   parsley

In large saucepan bring both to boiling. Add carrots. Reduce heat; simmer, uncovered, 10 minutes. Drop chilled Matzo Ball dough by rounded tablespoonfuls into simmering broth, making 8 balls. Cover; simmer 30 minutes. Do not lift lid. Sprinkle with parsley. Serves 8.

Swiss-Broccoli Soup

2 teaspoons instant
   chicken bouillon
   granules
1 10-ounce package
   frozen cut
   broccoli
2 cups milk

1 cup shredded
   process Swiss
   cheese (4 ounces)
1/8 teaspoon ground
   nutmeg
1/4 cup all-purpose
   flour

In saucepan heat bouillon granules in 1½ cups *water* till dissolved. Add broccoli; cover and cook for 8 to 10 minutes or till tender. Add milk, cheese, nutmeg, and dash *pepper*. Cook and stir till cheese melts. Combine flour and ½ cup cold *water;* stir into broccoli mixture. Cook and stir till thickened and bubbly. Makes 4 to 6 servings.

Mushroom-Barley Soup

8 ounces fresh mush-
   rooms, sliced
   (3 cups)
1 medium green
   pepper, chopped
   (½ cup)
1 medium onion,
   chopped (½ cup)
1 clove garlic, minced

2 tablespoons butter
   or margarine
3/4 cup quick-cooking
   barley
3/4 teaspoon ground
   sage
1/2 teaspoon salt
5 cups beef broth
   (see tip, page 174)

In 3-quart covered saucepan cook mushrooms, green pepper, onion, and garlic in butter or margarine about 5 minutes or till tender but not brown. Stir in barley, sage, and salt. Add broth; bring to boiling. Reduce heat; cover and simmer 20 to 25 minutes or till barley is tender. Makes 6 servings.

Creamy Celery-Zucchini Soup

3 cups sliced celery
3 green onions, finely
  chopped
2 tablespoons butter
1 medium zucchini
1 tablespoon instant
  chicken bouillon
  granules

1½ cups milk
1 tablespoon corn-
  starch
2 sprigs parsley,
  snipped

In 3-quart covered saucepan cook celery and onions in butter for 5 to 10 minutes. Meanwhile, cut zucchini in half lengthwise. Slice zucchini. Add zucchini, bouillon granules, 1 cup *water*, and ¼ teaspoon *salt* to saucepan. Cover; simmer 10 minutes. Blend milk and cornstarch; add to saucepan. Cook and stir till thickened and bubbly. Season to taste. Sprinkle parsley atop each serving. Makes 4 servings.

Tomato Tune-Up

3 cups tomato juice
½ cup sliced celery
2 thin slices onion
4 whole cloves
1 bay leaf
2 dashes bottled hot
  pepper sauce

1 10½-ounce can
  condensed beef
  broth
⅓ cup dry white wine

In saucepan combine tomato juice, celery, onion, cloves, bay leaf, and pepper sauce. Bring to boiling. Reduce heat; cover and simmer 20 minutes. Strain soup, discarding seasonings. Return soup to saucepan; add condensed broth and wine. Return to boiling. Float a thin lemon slice in each bowl, if desired. Makes 8 servings.

Celery-Spinach Soup

1 10¾-ounce can
condensed
chicken broth
1 10-ounce package
frozen spinach
2 cups chopped celery
1 cup chopped onion

1 cup cream-style
cottage cheese
2 cups milk
½ teaspoon salt
⅛ teaspoon pepper
½ cup dairy sour
cream

In 3-quart saucepan combine condensed broth, frozen spinach, celery, and onion. Bring to boiling. Reduce heat; cover and simmer 10 minutes or till vegetables are tender. Transfer to blender container; add cottage cheese. Cover and blend till smooth. Return mixture to saucepan. Stir in milk, salt, and pepper; heat through. Top each serving with a dollop of sour cream. Makes 6 servings.

Cheese-Spinach Soup

½ cup chopped onion
½ cup chopped celery
¼ cup butter *or*
margarine
¼ cup all-purpose
flour
½ teaspoon salt
⅛ teaspoon pepper

4 cups milk
1 10-ounce package
frozen chopped
spinach, thawed
1½ cups shredded
American cheese
(6 ounces)

In 3-quart saucepan cook onion and celery in butter or margarine till onion is tender. Stir in flour, salt, and pepper. Add milk all at once; cook and stir till thickened and bubbly. Stir in spinach and cheese; cook and stir till cheese melts. Makes 4 to 6 servings.

Butternut Squash and Apple Soup

This unusual soup uses bread crumbs as its thickener—

1 small butternut
  squash, halved
  and seeded
  (16 ounces)

3 medium green
  apples, peeled,
  cored, and
  coarsely chopped
  (3 cups)

2 10¾-ounce cans
  condensed
  chicken broth

1½ cups water

3 slices white bread,
  torn into pieces

1 medium onion,
  chopped (½ cup)

1 teaspoon salt

¼ teaspoon dried rose-
  mary, crushed

¼ teaspoon dried
  marjoram,
  crushed

⅛ teaspoon freshly
  ground pepper

¼ cup whipping cream
  Snipped parsley

Peel and cut up squash. In 4-quart Dutch oven combine the squash, apples, condensed chicken broth,
water, bread, onion, salt, rosemary, marjoram, and
pepper. Bring to boiling. Reduce heat; simmer, uncovered, for 45 minutes. Turn *one-fourth* of the soup mixture into a blender container. Cover and blend till
smooth; set aside. Repeat with remaining mixture,
one-fourth at a time. Return all the soup to the Dutch
oven. Bring to boiling. Reduce heat to simmering. Stir
in cream. Garnish each serving with snipped parsley.
Makes 6 to 8 servings.

Mexicali Bean Soup

½ cup chopped onion
1 clove garlic, minced
2 tablespoons cooking oil
2 16-ounce cans red kidney beans, drained
1 16-ounce can tomatoes, cut up
1 16-ounce can cream-style corn

1 4-ounce can green chili peppers, rinsed, seeded and chopped
1 tablespoon instant chicken bouillon granules
1 teaspoon ground cumin
Puffy Cheese Noodles (see recipe, page 178)

In 5-quart Dutch oven cook onion and garlic in oil till onion is tender. Stir in cooking oil, kidney beans, tomatoes, corn, chili peppers, bouillon granules, 6 cups *water*, 2 teaspoons *salt*, and ¼ teaspoon *pepper*. Cover and simmer 25 minutes. Add Puffy Cheese Noodles; simmer, uncovered, 10 to 12 minutes or till noodles are done. Serves 6 to 8.

Micro-Cooking

A countertop microwave oven saves time in preparing soups and stews. Use it for a single preparation step, such as melting butter, cooking onion in butter, or cooking bacon (see timings below). Or, use it to prepare entire recipes (see Index—Microwave Cooking).

For all recipes in this book, use the high-power setting of a countertop microwave oven. Use only nonmetal containers.

• Cook ½ cup chopped onion in 1 tablespoon butter, covered, 2 to 3 minutes; stir once.
• Cook 4 slices bacon between layers of paper toweling in a shallow dish, about 3 minutes.

Turn-About Gazpacho

Use a food processor if you like, but process only one-third of the vegetable mixture at a time—

1 16-ounce can tomatoes

1 10½-ounce can *condensed* beef broth

1 small cucumber, cut up

2 stalks celery, sliced (1 cup)

½ medium green pepper, cut up

4 sprigs parsley

¼ cup sliced green onion

¼ teaspoon garlic salt

¼ teaspoon freshly ground pepper

Dash bottled hot pepper sauce

5 or 6 pats butter *or* margarine

1 cup plain *or* seasoned croutons

In blender container combine *half each* of the tomatoes, beef broth, and cucumber. Cover and blend till slightly chopped. Add *half each* of the celery, green pepper, and parsley. Blend just till vegetables are coarsely chopped; pour into a 2-quart saucepan. Repeat with remaining tomatoes, broth, cucumber, celery, green pepper, and parsley. (Or, coarsely chop vegetables by hand.) Stir in green onion, garlic salt, pepper, and bottled hot pepper sauce. Cover and simmer 18 to 20 minutes or till vegetables are barely tender. Top each serving with a pat of butter or margarine and sprinkle with croutons. Makes 5 or 6 servings.

Cream of Fresh Vegetable Soup

1½ cups chicken broth
    (see tip, page 174)
½ cup chopped onion
    Desired vegetable
    and seasonings
    (see chart pages
    28–29)

2 tablespoons butter
2 tablespoons all-
    purpose flour
½ teaspoon salt
    Few dashes white
    pepper
1 cup milk

In saucepan combine chicken broth, chopped onion, and one of the vegetable-seasoning combinations from chart. (Or, substitute an equal amount of frozen vegetable, if desired.) Bring mixture to boiling. Reduce heat; cover and simmer the time indicated in the chart or till vegetable is tender. (Remove bay leaf if using broccoli.)

Place *half* the vegetable mixture into a blender container or food processor. Cover and blend 30 to 60 seconds or till smooth. Pour into bowl. Repeat with remaining vegetable mixture; set all aside.

In the same saucepan melt the butter. Blend in flour, salt, and pepper. Add the milk all at once. Cook and stir till mixture is thickened and bubbly. Stir in the blended vegetable mixture. Cook and stir till soup is heated through. Season to taste with additional salt and pepper. Serves 3 or 4.

Vegetable	Seasonings	Cooking Time	Yield
2 cups cut asparagus	1 teaspoon lemon juice ⅛ teaspoon ground mace	8 minutes	3½ cups
1½ cups cut green beans	½ teaspoon dried savory, crushed	20 to 30 minutes	3 cups
2 cups cut broccoli	½ teaspoon dried thyme, crushed 1 small bay leaf Dash garlic powder	10 minutes	3½ cups
1 cup sliced carrots	1 tablespoon snipped parsley ½ teaspoon dried basil, crushed	12 minutes	3½ cups
2 cups sliced cauliflower	½ to ¾ teaspoon curry powder	10 minutes	3½ cups
1½ cups chopped celery	2 tablespoons snipped parsley ½ teaspoon dried basil, crushed	15 minutes	3 cups

Vegetable	Seasonings	Cooking Time	Yield
1 cup sliced fresh mushrooms	1/8 teaspoon ground nutmeg	5 minutes	2⅔ cups
1½ cups shelled peas	1/4 cup shredded lettuce 2 tablespoons diced fully cooked ham 1/4 teaspoon dried sage, crushed	8 minutes	3½ cups
1 cup sliced potatoes	1/2 teaspoon dried dillweed	10 minutes	3 cups
4 medium tomatoes, peeled, quartered, and seeded	1/4 teaspoon dried basil, crushed	15 minutes	3⅓ cups
1½ cups cut unpeeled zucchini	Several dashes ground nutmeg	5 minutes	3⅓ cups

QUICK SOUPS

HOT SOUPS

Oyster-Spinach Soup

　2　cups milk
　2　10¾-ounce cans condensed cream of chicken soup
　2　9- *or* 10-ounce packages frozen chopped spinach
　　　in cream sauce
　2　8-ounce cans oysters
　1　cup dry white wine
　¼　teaspoon white pepper

In saucepan or Dutch oven stir milk into condensed soup. Remove spinach from pouches; add to soup. Cook and stir over medium heat, breaking up spinach with a fork till thawed; simmer, uncovered, 10 minutes, stirring occasionally. Stir in *undrained* oysters, wine, and pepper. Cook and stir till heated through. Garnish with lemon slices, if desired. Makes 8 servings.

Spaghetti-Corn Soup

1 envelope *regular* onion soup mix
2 15-ounce cans spaghetti rings with meatballs in
   tomato sauce
1 16-ounce can cream-style corn
   Grated parmesan cheese

Prepare onion soup mix according to package directions. Stir in spaghetti and meatballs and corn; heat through. Serve with grated parmesan. Makes 8 servings.

Caldo Con Queso

2½ cups water
2 canned green chili
   peppers, seeded
   and cut up
1 tomato, peeled and
   diced
½ teaspoon garlic salt
¼ teaspoon pepper
   • • •
1 13-ounce can (1⅔
   cups) evaporated
   milk

1 10¾-ounce can
   condensed cream
   of potato soup
1 10¾-ounce can
   condensed cream
   of onion soup
8 ounces monterey
   jack cheese

In 3-quart saucepan combine water, green chili peppers, tomato, garlic salt, and pepper. Bring to boiling. Reduce heat; cover and simmer 5 minutes. Blend in evaporated milk, condensed cream of potato soup, and condensed cream of onion soup. Heat through.

Meanwhile, cut the monterey jack cheese into small cubes; divide cheese cubes evenly among soup bowls. Ladle hot soup over cheese; serve immediately. Makes 6 to 8 servings.

Sun's Up Soup

    2 cups milk
    1 10¾-ounce can condensed cream of potato soup
    ½ of a 3-ounce package sliced smoked beef, snipped
    ½ cup shredded American cheese (2 ounces)
    1 slice bread, toasted and cut into triangles

In 2-quart saucepan gradually stir milk into soup; add smoked beef and cheese. Cook and stir about 5 minutes or till mixture is heated through. Top each serving with a toast triangle. Makes 4 servings.

Portuguese Ham and Egg Soup

    1 10½-ounce can condensed chicken with rice soup
    1 soup can water (1¼ cups)
    ¼ cup finely chopped fully cooked ham
    2 green onions, thinly sliced
    2 teaspoons lemon juice
    1 beaten egg
       Ground nutmeg

In saucepan heat soup and water according to label directions; add ham, onions, and lemon juice. Stir about *half* the hot mixture into beaten egg; return to saucepan. Heat and stir till mixture simmers. Sprinkle lightly with nutmeg. Makes 4 servings.

Appetizer Broccoli Soup

2 10-ounce packages frozen chopped broccoli
2 10¾-ounce cans condensed cream of mushroom
   soup
2 soup cans milk (2½ cups)
½ cup dry white wine
¼ cup butter *or* margarine
½ teaspoon dried tarragon, crushed
   Dash white pepper

In large saucepan cook broccoli according to package directions; drain. Add soup, milk, wine, butter or margarine, tarragon, and pepper. Heat through. Makes 8 servings.

Corn-Peanut Chowder

2 cups water
1 envelope *regular* chicken noodle soup mix
1 tablespoon finely chopped onion
¼ teaspoon salt
2 cups milk
1 16-ounce can cream-style corn
2 tablespoons creamy peanut butter

In 3-quart saucepan bring water to boiling; add soup mix, onion, and salt. Reduce heat; cover and simmer about 10 minutes or till noodles are tender. Stir in milk, corn, and peanut butter; heat through. Serves 4 to 6.

Shortcut Minestrone

4 slices bacon, cut up
1 envelope *regular* tomato-vegetable soup mix
4 cups water
1 18-ounce can red kidney beans, drained
1 10-ounce package frozen mixed vegetables
    Grated parmesan cheese

In 3-quart saucepan cook bacon till crisp; drain and set aside. In same saucepan blend together dry soup mix, water, beans, and mixed vegetables. Bring to boiling. Reduce heat; cover and simmer 10 to 15 minutes. Pass the cooked bacon and grated parmesan to sprinkle atop. Makes 5 or 6 servings.

Serving Dishes

When choosing serving dishes, consider the soup you're preparing. Chunky soups are attractive in shallow or deep soup bowls. Knife-and-fork soups and stews require shallow soup plates. Drink soups without solid pieces from mugs or cups, if you like. And for lunches away from home, don't forget wide-mouthed vacuum containers to keep soup hot.

In the kitchen, ladle soup right from the kettle. Or, serve it at the table from a tureen or casserole.

Salami-Bean Chowder

2 cups water
2 stalks celery, chopped (1 cup)
4 ounces salami, cut into small chunks (about ¾ cup)
1 medium onion, chopped (½ cup)
1 16-ounce can pork and beans in tomato sauce
1 10¾-ounce can condensed tomato soup
1 teaspoon worcestershire sauce

In medium saucepan combine water, celery, salami, and onion; bring to boiling. Reduce heat; cover and simmer 15 minutes. Stir in remaining ingredients; heat through. Makes 6 servings.

Egg-Lemon Soup

1 envelope *regular* chicken noodle soup mix
2 tablespoons cold water
1 tablespoon cornstarch
2 eggs
2 tablespoons lemon juice

Prepare soup mix according to package directions. Blend water and cornstarch; stir into soup. Cook and stir till bubbly. In small mixer bowl beat eggs about 4 minutes or till light. Gradually stir in *1 cup* of the hot soup. Return all to saucepan. Stir in lemon juice. Cook, stirring constantly, 2 minutes. Serves 8.

COLD SOUPS

Gazpacho

An uncooked, cold soup—

4 large tomatoes
1 small cucumber, chopped (1 cup)
1 medium green pepper, chopped (½ cup)
1 stalk celery, chopped (½ cup)
1 small onion, finely chopped (¼ cup)
1 clove garlic, minced

1 13¾-ounce can chicken broth
2 tablespoons lemon juice
1 tablespoon cooking oil
1 teaspoon sugar
1 teaspoon salt
¼ teaspoon pepper
Dash bottled hot pepper sauce
Croutons

Plunge tomatoes into boiling water for 30 seconds to loosen skins; then immerse in cold water. Slip skins off. Coarsely chop tomatoes (you should have about 2½ cups).

In large bowl combine chopped tomatoes, cucumber, green pepper, celery, onion, and garlic. Stir in chicken broth, lemon juice, oil, sugar, salt, pepper, and hot pepper sauce. Cover; chill thoroughly. Garnish each serving with croutons. Serves 8 to 10.

Note: For a smoother soup, combine all ingredients except croutons as directed above. Place *half* the mixture at a time in blender container (or *one-third* of the mixture at a time in a food processor). Cover and blend till smooth. Chill and serve as above.

Buttermilk-Shrimp Bisque

1 teaspoon onion salt
2 teaspoons prepared
    mustard
½ teaspoon sugar
½ teaspoon dried
    dillweed
Dash bottled hot
    pepper sauce
4 cups buttermilk
1 4½-ounce can small
    shrimp, drained
    and deveined

1 small cucumber,
    chopped (1 cup)
½ cup chopped green
    pepper
½ cup chopped celery
1 2-ounce jar diced
    pimiento, drained
    (¼ cup)

In 1½-quart bowl mix onion salt, mustard, sugar, dill-weed, and hot pepper sauce. Stir in buttermilk, shrimp, cucumber, green pepper, celery, and pimiento. Cover; chill. Makes 8 to 10 servings.

Zucchini-Tomato Soup

½ cup chopped onion
½ cup chopped green
    pepper
¼ cup water
1 18-ounce can (2¼
    cups) tomato
    juice

2 medium zucchini,
    quartered length-
    wise and sliced
    (2 cups)
1 8-ounce can whole
    kernel corn,
    drained
¼ teaspoon salt
2 cups buttermilk

In 2-quart saucepan cook onion and green pepper in water, covered, about 5 minutes or till vegetables are tender. Add tomato juice, zucchini, corn, and salt. Simmer, covered, 30 minutes. Cool. Stir into butter-milk. Cover; chill. Makes 8 to 10 servings.

Golden Squash and Carrot Bisque

3 medium yellow
summer squash,
sliced (3 cups)
2 medium carrots,
sliced (1 cup)
1 medium onion,
chopped (½ cup)

1 13¾-ounce can
chicken broth
½ teaspoon salt
1 13-ounce can (1⅔
cups) evaporated
milk
Snipped parsley

In 2-quart saucepan combine sliced summer squash, carrots, onion, chicken broth, and salt. Bring to boiling. Reduce heat; cover and simmer for 15 to 20 minutes or till carrots are just tender. Turn *half* the mixture into blender container or food processor; cover and blend till smooth. Pour into bowl; repeat with remaining mixture. Stir in evaporated milk. Cover and chill. Sprinkle with snipped parsley. Makes 6 servings.

Microwave cooking directions: Use ingredients as listed above. In 2-quart nonmetal casserole combine squash, carrots, and onion; sprinkle with salt. Cook, covered with waxed paper, in countertop microwave oven on high power about 15 minutes or till vegetables are tender, stirring once.

In blender container or food processor combine *half* the cooked vegetables and *half* the chicken broth; cover and blend till mixture is smooth. Turn into a bowl. Repeat with remaining vegetables and broth. Stir in the evaporated milk. Cover and chill. Sprinkle with parsley.

Vichyssoise

Make this elegant first-course soup ahead of time using either chicken broth or White Stock—

2 leeks
1 small onion, sliced
2 tablespoons butter
  or margarine
  • • •
3 small potatoes,
  peeled and sliced
  (2½ cups)

2 cups chicken broth
  (see tip, page 174)
  or White Stock
  (see recipe, page
  175)
1 teaspoon salt
1½ cups milk
1 cup whipping cream
  Snipped chives

Remove tops from leeks; slice leeks (you should have about ⅔ cup). In 2-quart saucepan cook leeks and onion in butter or margarine till vegetables are tender but not brown. Stir in sliced potatoes, chicken broth or White Stock, and salt. Bring to boiling. Reduce heat; cover and simmer for 35 to 40 minutes or till potatoes are very tender.

Place *half* of the mixture in blender container or food processor; cover and blend till mixture is smooth. Pour into bowl. Repeat with remaining mixture. Return all mixture to saucepan; stir in milk. Season to taste with additional salt and white pepper. Bring to boiling, stirring frequently. Cool. Stir in whipping cream. Cover and chill thoroughly before serving. Garnish with snipped chives. Makes 4 to 6 servings.

Creamy Green Pepper Soup

1 medium green
   pepper, chopped
   (½ cup)
1 small onion,
   chopped (¼ cup)

¼ cup water
1 10¾-ounce can
   condensed cream
   of celery soup
1¾ cups milk

In 1½-quart covered saucepan cook green pepper and onion in water, till tender. Do not drain. Stir in condensed soup, then the milk. Heat through, stirring occasionally. Cover and chill thoroughly. Float green pepper rings atop, if desired. Makes 3 or 4 servings.

Curried Coconut Soup

1 small onion,
   chopped (¼ cup)
1 teaspoon curry
   powder
¼ cup water
3 cups milk

1 cup flaked coconut
2 whole cloves
½ teaspoon salt
2 beaten egg yolks
Toasted coconut
   (optional)

In a 2-quart saucepan cook onion and curry powder in water till onion is tender. Stir in milk, coconut, cloves, and salt. Simmer, covered, for 15 minutes. Strain mixture through a sieve. Stir about *1 cup* of the hot milk mixture into the egg yolks. Return to remaining milk mixture in saucepan. Cook and stir about 2 minutes or till mixture thickens slightly. Remove from heat; cover and chill. Garnish each serving with toasted coconut, if desired. Makes 4 to 6 servings.

Crab-Avocado Soup

This sophisticated soup is made smooth with a blender or a food processor. Remember it for a special occasion—

1 large apple, peeled and chopped (1 cup)	1 medium avocado, seeded, peeled, and cut up
1 stalk celery, finely chopped (½ cup)	1 7½-ounce can crab meat, drained, flaked, and cartilage removed
1 tablespoon butter *or* margarine	
1 tablespoon all-purpose flour	½ cup light cream
2 cups chicken broth (see tip, page 174)	Salt
	Pepper
	Snipped chives

In medium saucepan cook apple and celery in butter or margarine about 5 minutes or till apple and celery are tender. Stir in the flour. Add chicken broth all at once; cook and stir till mixture is thickened and bubbly.

Place *half* the mixture in blender container or food processor. Add *half* the avocado. Cover and blend till smooth. Pour into bowl. Repeat with remaining broth mixture and avocado. Stir in the crab meat and light cream. Season to taste with some salt and pepper. Cover and chill. Before serving, garnish each serving with snipped chives. Makes 6 to 8 servings.

Blender Broccoli Soup

½ cup water
2 teaspoons instant
   beef bouillon
   granules
1 10-ounce package
   frozen chopped
   broccoli

1 cup milk
1 cup light cream
¼ teaspoon onion salt
Dash pepper
Dash ground
   nutmeg

In saucepan heat water and bouillon granules to boiling; add broccoli. Cover and simmer mixture for 3 minutes. Do not drain.

In blender container or food processor combine *half* the broccoli mixture and *half* the milk. Cover and blend till broccoli is very fine. Add *half* the cream, the onion salt, pepper, and nutmeg. Cover and blend about 1 minute or till smooth. Set mixture aside. Repeat with remaining broccoli, milk, and cream. Cover and chill. Stir before serving. If desired, garnish with sour cream and snipped chives. Makes 6 to 8 servings.

Serving Ideas for Cold Soups

Though traditionally thought of as appetizers, cold soups make tasty alternatives for refreshing snacks. They're great with a salad or sandwich for a summer lunch. And sweet fruit soups make delightful desserts or brunch fare.

Be sure to serve cold soups very cold in chilled mugs, cups, sherbet dishes, or bowls. Or, surround serving bowls with crushed ice in glass icers.

Since cold soups are usually not a main dish, offer ½- to ¾-cup servings.

Jellied Consommé

If using homemade beef broth, be sure that you clarify the broth before preparing this recipe—

4 cups beef broth (see tip, page 174)
2 tablespoons instant beef bouillon granules dissolved in 4 cups hot water
1 small onion, chopped (¼ cup)
½ of a medium green pepper, chopped (¼ cup)
1 tablespoon snipped parsley

1 teaspoon worcestershire sauce

• • •

2 tablespoons dry sherry
2 tablespoons water
1 envelope unflavored gelatin
½ cup whipping cream (optional)
¼ teaspoon curry powder (optional)

In saucepan combine beef broth, onion, green pepper, parsley, and worcestershire sauce. Bring to boiling. Reduce heat; simmer, uncovered, for 15 minutes to reduce liquid slightly (it should measure 3 to 3½ cups). Strain mixture, discarding vegetables. Return the strained broth to saucepan.

In small bowl combine sherry and water; sprinkle gelatin over liquid and let stand to soften gelatin. Stir gelatin mixture into broth; heat and stir till gelatin dissolves. Pour into a large bowl. Chill till set.

Before serving, whip cream and curry powder just to stiff peaks. Break up consommé with a fork; spoon into serving dishes. Top each serving with a dollop of the whipped cream. Makes 4 to 6 servings.

Asparagus Soup

¾ pound asparagus,
cut up *or* 1 10-
ounce package
frozen cut
asparagus

1 thin slice onion
½ cup boiling water
1 cup milk
½ cup light cream

In covered saucepan cook asparagus and onion slice in water 8 to 10 minutes or till crisp-tender; do not drain. Cool slightly. In blender container or food processor combine the undrained asparagus and onion, milk, cream, ½ teaspoon *salt*, and dash *pepper*. Cover and blend till smooth. Chill for 3 to 4 hours. Stir or blend before serving. Makes 4 to 6 servings.

Berry-Buttermilk Soup

2 cups fresh *or* frozen
loose-pack blue-
berries *or* straw-
berries
1½ cups water
½ cup sugar

½ teaspoon finely
shredded orange
peel
2 tablespoons orange
juice
2 cups buttermilk

Thaw berries, if frozen; drain. If desired, set aside 5 or 6 berries for garnish. In 1½-quart saucepan combine berries, water, sugar, orange peel, and juice. Bring to boiling. Reduce heat; cover and simmer 20 minutes. Cool 30 minutes.

Pour into blender container; cover and blend till smooth. Stir in the buttermilk. Cover and chill thoroughly. If desired, garnish each serving with a reserved berry or a thin orange slice. Makes 5 or 6 servings.

Cucumber-Cream Soup

3 medium cucumbers,
     peeled, seeded,
     and chopped
     (3 cups)
1 small onion,
     chopped (¼ cup)
3 tablespoons butter
     or margarine

¼ cup all-purpose
     flour
3 cups chicken broth
     (see tip, page 174)
1 cup whipping
     cream

In 2-quart saucepan cook cucumbers and onion, covered, in butter or margarine about 15 minutes or till tender. Stir in flour. Add chicken broth and whipping cream; cook and stir till thickened and bubbly. Pour *half* the mixture into blender container or food processor. Cover and blend till mixture is smooth. Set aside. Repeat with remaining mixture. Cover and chill. Garnish with additional cucumber slices, if desired. Makes 10 to 12 servings.

Microwave cooking directions: Use ingredients as listed above. In a 2-quart nonmetal bowl or casserole place cucumbers, onion, and butter or margarine. Cover with waxed paper and cook in a countertop microwave oven on high power about 7 minutes or till onion is tender. Stir in flour. Add chicken broth and cream. Cover and micro-cook 8 minutes or till thickened and bubbly, stirring every 2 minutes. Blend *half* the mixture in blender container or food processor till smooth. Set aside; repeat with remaining. Cover and chill. Serve as directed above.

Apple-Raisin Soup

2 cups apple juice *or* cider
2 large cooking apples, peeled and cubed (2 cups)

¼ cup light raisins
2 inches stick cinnamon
1 tablespoon brown sugar
1 tablespoon brandy

In 2-quart saucepan combine apple juice or cider, apples, raisins, and cinnamon. Cover; simmer 15 minutes or till apples are tender. Stir in sugar and brandy. Cover; chill. Remove stick cinnamon before serving. Makes 3 or 4 servings.

Creamy Fruit Soup

1 10-ounce package frozen raspberries, blueberries, strawberries, peaches, *or* mixed fruit, thawed
1 cup water
¼ cup sugar
2 inches stick cinnamon
Dash ground nutmeg

Dash ground cloves
1 tablespoon water
1 tablespoon cornstarch
2 tablespoons lemon juice
1 cup dairy sour cream
½ cup milk

Drain fruit, reserving syrup (cut up large pieces of fruit). In 1½-quart saucepan combine reserved syrup, the 1 cup water, sugar, cinnamon, nutmeg, and cloves. Bring to boiling; reduce heat and simmer, uncovered, for 5 minutes. Remove stick cinnamon. Blend the 1 tablespoon water and cornstarch; stir into saucepan. Cook and stir till thickened and bubbly. Remove from heat. Add lemon juice. Cool to room temperature. Blend in sour cream and fruit. Stir in milk. Cover and chill. Garnish with strips of lemon peel, if desired. Makes 4 to 6 servings.

Chilled Pea Soup

2 cups fresh *or* 1 10-
ounce package
frozen peas
2 cups shredded
lettuce
1 13¾-ounce can
chicken broth
⅓ cup water
¼ cup tomato juice
¼ cup finely chopped
green onion

1 tablespoon snipped
parsley
½ teaspoon salt
¼ teaspoon white
pepper
¼ teaspoon dried
thyme, crushed
½ cup whipping cream

In 2-quart saucepan combine peas, lettuce, chicken broth, water, tomato juice, onion, parsley, salt, white pepper, and thyme. Bring to boiling. Reduce heat; cover and simmer 20 minutes. Turn into blender container; cover and blend till smooth. Cool slightly; stir in whipping cream. Cover and chill. If desired, garnish with sour cream and fresh mint. Makes 4 servings.

Cherry-Wine Soup

1 16-ounce can pitted
tart red cherries
1½ cups water
½ cup sugar
1 tablespoon quick-
cooking tapioca

⅛ teaspoon ground
cloves
½ cup dry red wine

In 1½-quart saucepan stir together *undrained* cherries, water, sugar, tapioca, and cloves. Let stand 5 minutes. Bring to boiling. Reduce heat; cover and simmer for 15 minutes, stirring occasionally. Remove from heat; stir in wine. Cover and chill, stirring occasionally. Makes 6 to 8 servings.

QUICK SOUPS

COLD SOUPS

Cottage Cheese-Tomato Soup

  2 cups tomato juice
  1 cup cream-style cottage cheese
  ⅓ cup milk
  2 teaspoons soy sauce
  1 teaspoon worcestershire sauce
    Few drops bottled hot pepper sauce
  2 tablespoons sliced green onion

In blender container combine tomato juice, cottage cheese, milk, soy sauce, worcestershire sauce, and hot pepper sauce. Add *half* the green onion. Cover and blend till smooth. Cover and chill. Sprinkle individual servings with the remaining green onion. Makes 4 to 6 servings.

Pumpkin Bisque

  1 16-ounce can pumpkin
  ⅓ cup sour cream dip with chives
  2 cups chicken broth (see tip, page 174)
  1 cup light cream
  ½ teaspoon salt

In a mixing bowl combine pumpkin, sour cream dip, chicken broth, cream, and salt; beat smooth with rotary beater. Cover and chill. Garnish with dollops of additional sour cream dip with chives, if desired. Makes 6 to 8 servings.

Chilled Beet Soup

Served in glasses, teacups, mugs, or bowls, this ruby red soup makes a perfect appetizer or snack for a warm day. Garnish with lemon and green onion—

  1 16-ounce can diced
    beets
  1 slice onion
  1½ cups chicken broth
    (see tip, page 174)
  1 tablespoon lemon
    juice
  1 teaspoon sugar
  ½ teaspoon salt
  ¼ teaspoon pepper
  Dash ground cloves
  Lemon slices
    (optional)
  Sliced green onion
    (optional)

Combine the *undrained* beets and onion slice in blender container or food processor. Cover and blend till very smooth. In large bowl combine beet mixture, chicken broth, lemon juice, sugar, salt, pepper, and ground cloves; mix well.

Cover and chill thoroughly. Serve the soup in chilled bowls; top each serving with lemon slices and green onion, if desired. Makes 6 to 8 servings.

Blackberry Soup

1 16-ounce can blackberries
1 cup water
1 8-ounce carton lemon yogurt
½ cup grape juice
⅛ teaspoon ground cinnamon
1 small banana, sliced
2 tablespoons toasted coconut

Place *undrained* berries in blender container or food processor; cover and blend till smooth. Drain; discard seeds. Return liquid to blender or food processor; add water, yogurt, grape juice, and cinnamon. Cover and blend just till smooth. Cover and chill. Garnish with banana slices and toasted coconut. Makes 6 to 8 servings.

Appetizer Tomato Soup

1 10¾-ounce can condensed tomato soup
1¾ cups milk
1 8-ounce carton plain yogurt
1 teaspoon worcestershire sauce
¼ teaspoon celery salt
⅛ teaspoon onion powder

In bowl blend tomato soup, milk, yogurt, worcestershire sauce, celery salt, and onion powder. Cover; chill thoroughly. Top each serving with additional yogurt, if desired. Makes 6 servings.

Avocado Soup

1 13¾-ounce can chicken broth
2 medium avocados, seeded, peeled, and cut into
    chunks
2 tablespoons dry sherry
½ teaspoon salt
¼ teaspoon onion powder
⅛ teaspoon dried dillweed
¾ cup light cream

In blender container combine chicken broth, avocado chunks, dry sherry, salt, onion powder, and dillweed. Cover; blend till mixture is smooth. Stir in light cream. Cover; chill well. Top each serving with avocado slices or dollops of dairy sour cream, if desired. Makes 6 servings.

Tomato Soup Shake

1 10¾-ounce can condensed tomato soup
1 cup light cream
1 egg (optional)
¼ teaspoon ground nutmeg
  Milk

Combine condensed soup, cream, egg (if desired), and nutmeg in blender container or shaker. Blend or shake till smooth. Cover; chill. Thin with a little milk, if necessary. Serve in chilled cups or mugs. Makes 3 or 4 servings.

Orange-Apricot Soup

2 17-ounce cans apricot halves
1 teaspoon finely shredded orange peel
½ cup orange juice
¼ teaspoon ground cardamom
1 8-ounce carton plain yogurt

Drain apricots, reserving syrup. In blender container place reserved syrup and *half* the apricots. Add orange peel, juice, and cardamom. Cover and blend till smooth. Add yogurt; blend just till combined. Cut up remaining apricots; stir in. Cover and chill. Garnish with orange slices, if desired. Serves 8 to 10.

Shortcut Work with Appliances

Put your kitchen appliances to work and speed up soup-making tasks. For instance, use a blender or food processor to puree, chop, or blend foods. A food processor can slice and shred ingredients, as well.

A word of caution! Always read and follow the information in your appliances' use and care booklets. Be aware of the type and size of the food pieces you're processing, as well as the quantity that can be added to the appliance container at one time. You'll find that you may need to process the food in batches to prevent spills and overflow.

Chilly Celery Soup

  1 10¾-ounce can condensed cream of celery soup
1½ cups milk
  2 tablespoons chopped green pepper
  2 tablespoons diced pimiento
     Celery leaves

In blender container or food processor place celery soup and milk. Cover and blend till well mixed. Add green pepper and pimiento; cover and blend till finely chopped. Cover and chill thoroughly. Garnish each serving with celery leaves. Makes 3 or 4 servings.

Cantaloupe Mist

1 medium cantaloupe
¼ teaspoon ground cinnamon
1 6-ounce can frozen orange juice concentrate
2 juice cans water (about 1½ cups)
1 tablespoon lime juice

Cut cantaloupe in half and remove seeds. Scoop pulp into blender container or food processor. Add cinnamon. Cover and blend till smooth. Turn into large bowl. In same blender container or food processor place orange juice and water. Cover and blend till mixed. Stir into melon mixture; stir in lime juice. Cover and chill thoroughly. Stir before serving. Garnish with fresh mint leaves or lime wedges, if desired. Makes 6 to 8 servings.

WHOLE-MEAL SOUPS AND STEWS

Meat & Poultry—Fish & Seafood—Vegetable

Look to this chapter for main-dish soups and stews that can handle big or small appetites. First you'll find soups featuring beef, chicken, sausage, veal, lamb, and pork. Following these are plain and fancy soups that use fish and shellfish.

The vegetable section includes a selection of soups and stews that don't depend on meat for their protein power. Included are favorite bean, lentil, and pea soups.

MEAT AND POULTRY

Basic Stew

Use this recipe to make many stews by varying the meat, vegetables, and seasonings—

1½ pounds stew meat, cut into 1-inch cubes (beef, pork, lamb, *or* veal)

2 tablespoons cooking oil

1 clove garlic, minced

1 bay leaf

1 teaspoon salt

1 teaspoon prepared mustard *or* prepared horseradish

½ teaspoon dried herb, crushed (basil, oregano, marjoram, *or* thyme)

¼ teaspoon pepper

1 10½- *or* 10¾-ounce can condensed broth (beef *or* chicken)

5 cups fresh vegetables cut into 1-inch pieces (any combination of peeled potatoes, carrots, celery, rutabagas, turnips, onions, parsnips, *or* green peppers)

¼ cup cold water

2 tablespoons all-purpose flour

In large saucepan brown meat, *half* at a time, in hot oil. Return all meat to pan. Stir in garlic, bay leaf, salt, mustard or horseradish, herb, and pepper. Add the condensed beef or chicken broth. Bring to boiling. Reduce heat; cover and simmer till meat is nearly tender (about 30 minutes for pork, lamb, or veal; about 1¼ hours for beef). Add vegetables. Cover and simmer about 30 minutes or till meat and vegetables are tender. Blend water and flour; stir into stew. Cook and stir till thickened and bubbly. Remove bay leaf. Makes 6 servings.

Cider Stew

2 pounds beef stew meat, cut into 1-inch cubes
3 tablespoons all-purpose flour
2 teaspoons salt
¼ teaspoon pepper
¼ teaspoon dried thyme, crushed
3 tablespoons cooking oil

2 cups apple cider or apple juice
1 to 2 tablespoons vinegar
3 potatoes, peeled and quartered
4 carrots, quartered
2 onions, sliced
1 stalk celery, sliced

Coat meat with mixture of flour, salt, pepper, and thyme. In 4½-quart Dutch oven brown meat, *half* at a time, in hot oil. Drain off fat. Return all meat to Dutch oven. Stir in apple cider or juice, vinegar, and ½ cup *water;* cook and stir till mixture boils. Reduce heat; cover and simmer about 1¼ hours or till meat is nearly tender. Stir in vegetables. Cook 30 minutes more or till vegetables are done. Serves 6 to 8.

Crockery cooking directions: Use ingredients as listed above *except* add 1 *apple,* chopped; ½ cup cold *water;* and ¼ cup all-purpose *flour* as directed below. Coat meat with mixture of the 3 tablespoons flour, salt, pepper, and thyme. In skillet brown meat, *half* at a time, in hot oil. Drain off fat. Place vegetables and 1 *apple,* chopped, in electric slow crockery cooker. Place meat atop. Pour apple cider or juice and vinegar over meat. Cover and cook on low-heat setting for 10 to 12 hours. Turn cooker to high-heat setting. Blend ½ cup cold *water* and ¼ cup all-purpose *flour;* stir into stew. Cover and cook 15 minutes or till thickened. Season to taste.

Shaker Beef Goulash

2 tablespoons all-
   purpose flour
2 teaspoons salt
1/8 teaspoon pepper
2 pounds beef stew
   meat, cut into
   1-inch cubes
2 tablespoons cooking
   oil
2 large onions, sliced
1 cup water
1 cup apple juice *or*
   cider
2 medium rutabagas,
   peeled and
   chopped (4 cups)

6 medium carrots,
   chopped (3 cups)
2 tablespoons snipped
   parsley
1 teaspoon salt
1/2 teaspoon dried mar-
   joram, crushed
1/2 teaspoon dried
   thyme, crushed
1/3 cup cold water
3 tablespoons all-
   purpose flour
6 small potatoes,
   peeled, cooked,
   and mashed

In paper or plastic bag combine the 2 tablespoons flour, the 2 teaspoons salt, and the pepper. Add meat cubes, a few at a time, shaking to coat. In Dutch oven brown meat, *half* at a time, in hot oil. Return all meat to Dutch oven. Add onions, the 1 cup water, and apple juice. Cover and simmer about 1 1/4 hours or till meat is nearly tender. Add rutabagas, carrots, parsley, the 1 teaspoon salt, the marjoram, and thyme. Cover and simmer 30 minutes or till meat and vegetables are done. Blend the 1/3 cup water and the 3 tablespoons flour; stir into stew. Cook and stir till bubbly. Transfer to serving dish. Spoon potatoes around edge. Sprinkle with more parsley, if desired. Serves 8.

Chili Beef Soup

1½ pounds beef stew meat, cut into ½-inch cubes

2 tablespoons cooking oil

1 medium onion, chopped (½ cup)

1 medium green pepper, chopped (½ cup)

1 clove garlic, minced

• • •

3 cups water

1 18-ounce can (2¼ cups) tomato juice

1 16-ounce can tomatoes, cut up

1 16-ounce can whole kernel corn

1 15½-ounce can chili beans

2 bay leaves

1 tablespoon chili powder

2 teaspoons salt

1 teaspoon worcestershire sauce

¼ teaspoon pepper

¼ teaspoon crushed dried red pepper

½ cup cold water

⅓ cup all-purpose flour

In Dutch oven brown *half* the meat in hot oil; remove from pan. Brown the remaining meat with onion, green pepper, and garlic. Return all meat to pan. Add the 3 cups water, the tomato juice, *undrained* tomatoes, *undrained* corn, *undrained* chili beans, bay leaves, chili powder, salt, worcestershire sauce, pepper, and dried red pepper. Bring to boiling. Reduce heat; cover and simmer for 1½ to 2 hours or till meat is tender. Remove bay leaves.

Blend the ½ cup cold water and the flour. Stir into soup; cook and stir till slightly thickened and bubbly. Makes 8 servings.

Beef Stew with Ravioli Dumplings

3 tablespoons all-
   purpose flour
1 teaspoon salt
   Dash pepper
1 pound beef stew
   meat, cut into
   1-inch cubes
2 tablespoons cooking
   oil
1 medium onion,
   chopped (½ cup)

1 clove garlic, minced
¾ teaspoon dried
   oregano, crushed
1 10-ounce package
   frozen peas and
   carrots
1 15-ounce can beef
   ravioli in sauce
2 tablespoons snipped
   parsley

In paper or plastic bag combine flour, salt, and pepper. Add beef cubes, a few at a time, shaking to coat. In skillet brown meat quickly in hot oil. Add onion, garlic, and oregano; cook till onion is tender. Drain off fat. Add 2½ cups *water*. Cover and simmer about 1¼ hours or till meat is nearly tender. In strainer rinse peas and carrots under hot water to separate; stir peas and carrots, ravioli, and parsley into stew. Cover and cook 20 minutes longer. Makes 4 servings.

Crockery cooking directions: (Use 3½-quart or smaller electric slow crockery cooker because of small volume.) Use ingredients as listed above. Coat beef with mixture of flour, salt, and pepper. In skillet brown meat in hot oil. Add onion, garlic, and oregano; cook till onion is tender. Transfer to electric slow crockery cooker. Add peas and carrots and 1½ cups *water*. Cover and cook on low-heat setting for 8 to 10 hours. Turn cooker to high-heat setting. Stir in ravioli and parsley. Cover and cook 15 minutes or till heated through.

Spiced Beef Stew

2 pounds beef stew
meat, cut into
1-inch cubes
2 tablespoons cooking
oil
2½ cups water
1 10½-ounce can
condensed beef
broth
2 bay leaves
2 teaspoons dried
oregano, crushed
2 teaspoons ground
coriander
1½ teaspoons salt
1 teaspoon ground
cumin
¼ teaspoon pepper

1 clove garlic, minced
¾ cup cold water
½ cup all-purpose
flour
3 medium sweet pota-
toes, peeled and
cubed (about
3 cups)
2 medium tomatoes,
peeled and
quartered
1 medium onion, cut
into wedges
1 medium green pep-
per, cut into
strips
½ small head cabbage,
cut into wedges

In 4½-quart Dutch oven brown meat, *half* at a time, in hot oil. Return all meat to pan. Add the 2½ cups water, the condensed beef broth, bay leaves, oregano, coriander, salt, cumin, pepper, and garlic. Bring to boiling. Reduce heat; cover and simmer about 1¼ hours or till meat is nearly tender. Remove bay leaves; skim off fat. Blend together the ¾ cup water and flour; stir into meat mixture. Cook and stir till thickened and bubbly. Stir in sweet potatoes, tomatoes, onion, and green pepper; arrange cabbage atop. Cover and simmer about 20 minutes or till meat and vegetables are tender. Serves 8.

Beef and Bean Ragout

1 cup dry dark red kidney beans	1½ teaspoons salt
3 cups water	1 teaspoon sugar
¼ cup all-purpose flour	½ teaspoon dried thyme, crushed
½ teaspoon salt	⅛ teaspoon pepper
2 pounds beef stew meat, cut into 1-inch cubes	1 bay leaf
	3 medium potatoes, peeled and cubed (3 cups)
2 tablespoons cooking oil	
1 16-ounce can tomatoes, cut up	2 medium onions, cut into wedges
¾ cup dry red wine	1 medium green pepper, chopped (½ cup)
2 cloves garlic, minced	

Rinse beans. Place in 2-quart saucepan with the water; bring to boiling. Reduce heat and simmer 2 minutes. Remove from heat; cover and let stand 1 hour. (Or, combine beans and water; soak overnight.) *Do not drain.* Bring beans to boiling. Reduce heat, cover and simmer 45 minutes. Drain beans.

Combine flour and the ½ teaspoon salt; coat meat with flour mixture. In 4-quart Dutch oven brown meat, *half* at a time, in hot oil. Return all meat to pan. Add drained beans, *undrained* tomatoes, wine, garlic, the 1½ teaspoons salt, the sugar, thyme, pepper, and bay leaf to the meat. Bring to boiling; reduce heat. Cover and simmer about 1¼ hours or till meat is nearly tender. Add potatoes, onions, and green pepper. Cook 30 minutes more or till meat and potatoes are tender. Remove bay leaf. Makes 8 to 10 servings.

Beef Soup

Use acorn, butternut, hubbard, or other winter squash in this distinctive soup—

2 pounds beef flank
    steak
1 tablespoon lard *or*
    cooking oil
6 cups water
1 tablespoon salt
4 potatoes, peeled
    and quartered
2 carrots, cut into
    1-inch pieces
2 onions, quartered
8 ounces winter
    squash *or* pump-
    kin, peeled and
    cut into 8 pieces

2 ears fresh corn,
    quartered
1 cup sliced fresh
    green beans
¼ cup long grain rice
¼ cup chopped celery
    leaves
¼ cup snipped parsley
2 cloves garlic,
    minced
¼ teaspoon ground
    white pepper
⅛ teaspoon crushed
    dried red pepper

Cut meat into 8 pieces. In 5-quart Dutch oven brown meat, *half* at a time, in hot lard or cooking oil. Return all meat to pan; add the water and salt. Bring mixture to boiling. Reduce heat; cover and simmer about 1¼ hours or till meat is nearly tender. Add potatoes, carrots, onions, squash or pumpkin, corn, beans, uncooked rice, celery leaves, parsley, garlic, white pepper, and red pepper. Cover and simmer about 30 minutes or till vegetables are tender. Remove meat and vegetables to platter. Divide broth among 8 soup plates; add ingredients from platter. Makes 8 servings.

Succotash Soup

1½ pounds corned beef
    brisket
1 medium carrot,
    chopped (½ cup)
1 stalk celery,
    chopped (½ cup)
8 cups water
1 2½- to 3-pound
    broiler-fryer
    chicken, cut up
2 medium potatoes,
    peeled and
    chopped (2 cups)

2 cups fresh lima
    beans or 1 10-
    ounce package
    frozen lima beans
1 medium onion,
    chopped (½ cup)
½ teaspoon dried sage,
    crushed
¼ teaspoon pepper
4 ears corn or 1 10-
    ounce package
    frozen whole
    kernel corn

In 5-quart Dutch oven combine beef, carrot, and celery. Add water; bring to boiling. Reduce heat; cover and simmer for 1½ hours. Add chicken pieces; simmer, covered, for 45 to 50 minutes or till beef and chicken are tender. Remove beef and chicken; strain broth, discarding vegetables. Spoon fat from broth. Cool beef and chicken slightly. Remove and discard skin and bones from chicken. Cut up beef and chicken; set aside. Add potatoes, lima beans, onion, sage, and pepper to broth. Cover and simmer about 20 minutes or till limas are almost tender. Cut fresh corn from cobs. Stir fresh or frozen corn, beef, and chicken into soup. Return to boil. Cover and simmer about 15 minutes or till vegetables are tender. Season to taste with salt and pepper. Makes 8 to 10 servings.

Beef and Kraut Soup

2 pounds beef shank crosscuts	1 8-ounce can sauerkraut, snipped
2 tablespoons cooking oil	1 8-ounce can tomatoes, cut up
1 medium onion, chopped (½ cup)	1 medium apple, peeled, cored, and chopped
1 clove garlic, minced	
4 whole cloves	1 green pepper, chopped (½ cup)
1 bay leaf	
2 teaspoons salt	1 teaspoon sugar
⅛ teaspoon pepper	

In Dutch oven brown beef in hot oil. Remove from pan; add onion and garlic to drippings and cook till onion is tender. Return beef to pan. Add cloves, bay leaf, salt, pepper, and 4 cups *water*. Cover and simmer for 1½ hours. Remove beef. Remove bay leaf and cloves. When cool enough to handle, remove meat from bones; cut up meat and return to broth. Discard bones. Stir in *undrained* sauerkraut, *undrained* tomatoes, apple, green pepper, and sugar. Bring to boiling; reduce heat. Cover and simmer 15 to 20 minutes more or till pepper is tender. Top with sour cream, if desired. Makes 6 servings.

Crockery cooking directions: Use ingredients as listed above. In skillet brown beef in oil; drain. Transfer beef to electric slow crockery cooker. Combine remaining ingredients and 3 cups *water*. Pour mixture over beef in cooker. Cover and cook on low-heat setting about 10 hours. Remove beef; skim off any fat. Remove bay leaf and cloves. Remove meat from bones; cut up meat and return to soup. Discard bones.

Short Rib-Vegetable Stew

2 pounds beef short ribs, cut into serving-size pieces
1 tablespoon cooking oil
1 16-ounce can tomatoes, cut up
1 medium onion, chopped (½ cup)
1 clove garlic, minced
1½ teaspoons salt
1½ teaspoons instant vegetable bouillon granules

½ teaspoon dried basil, crushed
Dash pepper
1 pound tiny new potatoes (10 to 12)
3 carrots, cut into ½-inch pieces
1 8½-ounce can peas, drained
1 8½-ounce can lima beans, drained
2 tablespoons snipped parsley

Trim excess fat from ribs. In Dutch oven slowly brown ribs in hot oil on all sides; drain off fat. Add *undrained* tomatoes, onion, garlic, salt, bouillon granules, basil, and pepper. Add 2½ cups *water*. Bring to boiling. Reduce heat; cover and simmer for 2 hours or till meat is nearly tender. Skim off fat.

Peel strip around center of each potato, if desired. Add potatoes, carrots, drained peas, drained lima beans, and parsley to Dutch oven. Cover and simmer about 30 minutes more or till vegetables are tender. Season to taste with salt and pepper. Makes 6 servings.

Crockery cooking directions: Use ingredients as listed above. Trim excess fat from ribs. In skillet slowly brown ribs in hot oil on all sides; drain well. Combine *undrained* tomatoes, garlic, salt, bouillon granules, basil, and pepper. Set aside. Peel strip around center of each potato, if desired. Place potatoes, carrots, onion, peas, limas, and parsley in electric slow crockery cooker. Add browned ribs. Pour tomato mixture over meat in cooker. Add 2 cups *water:* do not stir. Cover and cook on low-heat setting for 8 hours. Skim off excess fat. Season to taste.

Crockery Cooker Hints

Electric slow crockery cookers come in three basic types: 1) cookers with heating wires wrapped entirely around the sides of the cooker, 2) cookers with heating elements in the bottom, and 3) cookers with a separate heating unit.

Cooking characteristics vary with each type, and we found that our recipes developed for unattended long-term cooking were satisfactory only when done in the first kind of cooker.

All the crockery cooking directions given in this book were tested only in cookers with heating elements wrapped around the sides. These pots have very low wattage and their heating element is on continuously. Foods in liquid can be left unattended for 8 or more hours without boiling dry or sticking. This group of pots can be identified by its heat control with one or two fixed settings, usually low and high.

Most of the recipe directions specify the low-heat setting. However, if you want to reduce the cooking time, most foods cook on the high-heat setting in half the time they require on the low-heat setting.

Meaty Minestrone

3 pounds beef shank
crosscuts
1 medium onion,
chopped (½ cup)
1 bay leaf
2 teaspoons salt
¼ teaspoon pepper
8 cups water
1 16-ounce can cut
green beans,
drained
1 15-ounce can gar-
banzo beans,
drained
1 8-ounce can toma-
toes, cut up

2 medium carrots,
thinly sliced
(1 cup)
4 ounces Polish sau-
sage, thinly sliced
2 ounces fine noodles
(1¼ cups)
2 tablespoons snipped
parsley
1 clove garlic, minced
1½ teaspoons dried
basil, crushed
Grated parmesan
cheese (optional)

In Dutch oven combine beef, onion, bay leaf, salt, and
pepper. Add water. Cover and simmer about 1½ hours
or till meat is tender. Remove beef; skim fat from
broth. When meat is cool enough to handle, remove
meat from bones; cut up meat and return to broth.
Discard bones. Add green beans, garbanzo beans, *undrained* tomatoes, carrots, sausage, noodles, parsley,
garlic, and basil to soup. Cover and simmer for 20 to
25 minutes or till vegetables and noodles are tender.
Remove bay leaf; season to taste. If desired, pass
grated parmesan cheese. Makes 8 to 10 servings.

Beef Stew with Wontons

1½ pounds beef stew
    meat, cut into
    1-inch cubes
1 medium onion,
    chopped (½ cup)
1 clove garlic, minced
2 tablespoons cooking
    oil
½ cup dry white wine
¼ cup soy sauce
2 teaspoons instant
    beef bouillon
    granules

2 teaspoons sugar
½ teaspoon ground
    ginger
    Wontons (see recipe
    below)
3 cups coarsely
    chopped bok choy
1 cup sliced fresh
    mushrooms
1 6-ounce package
    frozen pea pods
¼ cup cornstarch

In 4-quart Dutch oven cook meat, onion, and garlic,
half at a time, in oil till meat is brown. Return all to
pan. Add wine, soy, bouillon granules, sugar, ginger,
and 3½ cups *water*. Bring to boiling; reduce heat.
Cover and simmer 1½ hours or till meat is tender; stir
occasionally. Meanwhile, prepare Wontons.

Add bok choy, mushrooms, and pea pods to stew;
simmer 2 or 3 minutes. Blend cornstarch and ¼ cup
cold *water;* stir into hot mixture. Cook and stir till
thickened and bubbly. Add hot Wontons. Serves 6 to 8.

Wontons

1 4½-ounce can
  shrimp
1 beaten egg yolk
½ cup finely chopped
  bok choy
¼ cup finely chopped
  onion

1 tablespoon soy
  sauce
½ teaspoon sugar
¼ teaspoon ground
  ginger
20 wonton skins

Drain, devein, and chop shrimp. Combine shrimp, egg
yolk, bok choy, onion, soy, sugar, ginger, ¼ teaspoon
salt, and ⅛ teaspoon *pepper*. Follow directions below
for filling and wrapping wontons. In large saucepan
cook wontons in a large amount of boiling water for
3 to 5 minutes. Drain. Add to stew (see recipe above).

Wrapping Wontons

Buy wonton skins at the supermarket or Oriental food store. If wonton skins are not available, purchase egg roll skins and cut each in quarters.

Position wonton skin with one point toward you. Spoon a scant tablespoonful of filling just off center of skin. Fold bottom point of wonton

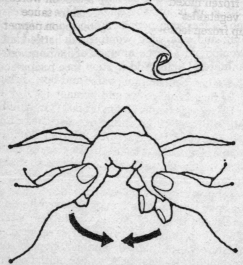

skin over filling; tuck point under filling, leaving about 1 inch unrolled at top of skin. Moisten right-hand corner of skin with water. Grasp right- and left-hand corners as shown; bring these corners toward you below the filling. Overlap left-hand corner over right-hand corner; press to seal.

Easy Vegetable-Beef Soup

Soup mix and frozen vegetables save you time when making this tasty soup—

5 cups water
1½ pounds beef shank crosscuts
1 16-ounce can tomatoes, cut up
1 10-ounce package frozen mixed vegetables
1 cup frozen loose-pack hash brown potatoes

¼ cup *regular* onion soup mix
¼ cup sliced celery
1 teaspoon sugar
1 teaspoon seasoned salt
½ teaspoon worcestershire sauce
⅛ teaspoon pepper
Dash bottled hot pepper sauce

In 3-quart saucepan combine water and beef; bring to boiling. Reduce heat; cover and simmer for 1½ to 2 hours or till meat is tender. Skim off fat. (Or, chill beef and broth till layer of fat forms; remove and discard fat.) Remove meat. Measure the cooking liquid; reserve 3 cups of the liquid to use in soup (save remaining cooking liquid for another use). When the meat is cool enough to handle, remove meat from bones; cut meat into bite-size pieces. Discard bones.

In saucepan combine the 3 cups reserved liquid, the meat, *undrained* tomatoes, mixed vegetables, potatoes, dry onion soup mix, celery, sugar, seasoned salt, worcestershire sauce, pepper, and hot pepper sauce. Bring to boiling. Reduce heat; cover and simmer for 15 to 20 minutes or till vegetables are tender. Serves 6.

Oxtail Vegetable Soup

Choose the meatiest oxtails for this hearty soup—

2 pounds oxtails, cut into 1½-inch lengths

3 tablespoons all-purpose flour

2 tablespoons cooking oil

1 16-ounce can tomatoes, cut up

1 10½-ounce can *condensed* beef broth

½ cup water

½ cup dry red wine

1 medium onion, chopped (½ cup)

1 teaspoon sugar

½ teaspoon salt

½ teaspoon dried thyme, crushed

¼ teaspoon pepper

1 bay leaf

4 medium carrots, cut into julienne strips (2 cups)

4 medium parsnips, peeled and cut into julienne strips (2 cups)

½ cup frozen peas

Trim fat from oxtails. Coat oxtails with flour. In Dutch oven brown oxtails in hot oil. Add *undrained* tomatoes, condensed beef broth, water, wine, onion, sugar, salt, thyme, pepper, and bay leaf. Bring to boiling. Reduce heat; cover and simmer 2 hours or till meat is just tender. Skim off fat. Add carrots and parsnips; cover and simmer 25 minutes. Stir in peas; cook 5 minutes more. Serve in soup plates. Makes 4 servings.

Onion Oxtail Stew

⅓ cup all-purpose
  flour
1 teaspoon salt
  Dash pepper
5 pounds oxtails, cut
  into 1½-inch
  lengths
¼ cup cooking oil
1 10½-ounce can
  condensed beef
  broth
1 cup water
1 cup dry white wine
1 large onion,
  chopped (1 cup)
1 tomato, peeled and
  chopped

1 large carrot, finely
  chopped
1 medium turnip,
  peeled and finely
  chopped (1 cup)
2 cloves garlic,
  minced
  Few sprigs parsley
1 bay leaf
½ teaspoon salt
  Dash pepper
2 cups pearl onions
  or frozen small
  whole onions
3 medium carrots,
  sliced (1½ cups)

Combine the flour, the 1 teaspoon salt, and dash pepper. Coat oxtails with flour mixture. In 10-quart Dutch oven slowly brown oxtails, *half* at a time, in hot oil, turning often; drain off excess fat. Return all meat to pan. Add condensed beef broth, water, ½ *cup* of the wine, the chopped onion, tomato, the chopped carrot, turnip, garlic, parsley, and bay leaf. Bring to boiling. Reduce heat; cover and simmer 1½ hours. Remove and discard parsley and bay leaf. Skim off fat. Return to boiling; reduce heat and stir in remaining ½ cup wine, the ½ teaspoon salt, and dash pepper. Cover and simmer for 30 minutes. Add pearl onions and sliced carrots; cover and simmer 20 to 25 minutes more. Makes 5 to 8 servings.

Oven-Style Borscht Stew

2 pounds beef short
  ribs, cut up
1 tablespoon cooking
  oil
4 medium carrots,
  sliced (2 cups)
3 medium turnips,
  peeled and cut
  into julienne strips
2 stalks celery, sliced
  (1 cup)
1 large onion, sliced
4 cups water
1 6-ounce can
  tomato paste

1 tablespoon salt
¼ teaspoon pepper
• • •
1 cup water
1 tablespoon sugar
1 tablespoon vinegar
2 medium beets,
  peeled and cut
  into julienne strips
1 small head cabbage,
  cut into 6 wedges
Dairy sour cream

In 4½-quart Dutch oven brown short ribs in hot oil.
Drain off fat. Add carrots, turnips, celery, and onion.
Combine the 4 cups water, the tomato paste, salt, and
pepper; pour over vegetables in Dutch oven. Cover
and bake in 350° oven for 2 hours. Skim off fat.

Combine the 1 cup water, the sugar, and vinegar;
add to meat mixture. Add beets; place cabbage atop
mixture, pushing partially into liquid. Cover and continue baking 1½ hours more. Serve in soup plates.
Pass sour cream to spoon atop each serving. Makes 6
servings.

Oven-Baked Beef Stew

¼ cup all-purpose
  flour
2 teaspoons salt
⅛ teaspoon pepper
1½ pounds beef stew
  meat, cut into
  1-inch cubes
3 *or* 4 medium car-
  rots, cut into
  2-inch strips
4 small onions,
  quartered
2 cups water
1 6-ounce can tomato
  paste

1 tablespoon vinegar
1 teaspoon sugar
⅛ teaspoon dried
  thyme, crushed
1 clove garlic, minced
1 bay leaf
1 10-ounce package
  frozen peas,
  broken apart
1 package refriger-
  ated biscuits
  (6 biscuits)
Milk
¼ cup crisp rice
  cereal, crushed

In paper or plastic bag combine flour, salt, and pepper. Add beef cubes, a few at a time; shake to coat.
Place coated beef cubes in a 2½-to-3-quart casserole;
add carrots and onions. In bowl combine water, tomato paste, vinegar, sugar, thyme, garlic, and bay leaf;
pour over meat mixture in casserole. Bake, covered, in
350° oven for 2 hours.

Stir frozen peas into stew mixture; cover and bake
20 minutes longer. Remove casserole from oven; discard bay leaf. Increase oven temperature to 425°.

Meanwhile, quarter the refrigerated biscuits; dip
each quarter in milk, then roll in cereal. Place atop hot
stew. Bake, uncovered, in 425° oven about 12 minutes
or till biscuits are done. Makes 6 servings.

Meatball Stew with Spinach Dumplings

1 beaten egg
¾ cup soft bread
  crumbs (1 slice)
1 teaspoon garlic salt
1 pound ground beef
1 tablespoon cooking
  oil
1 medium onion,
  chopped (½ cup)
1 11-ounce can con-
  densed cheddar
  cheese soup
1 soup can milk
  (1¼ cups)

1 16-ounce can diced
  beets, drained
1 10-ounce package
  frozen brussels
  sprouts
1 8-ounce can
  spinach, well-
  drained and
  chopped
1 cup packaged
  biscuit mix
¼ cup milk

Mix egg, crumbs, and garlic salt. Add beef; mix well. Shape meat mixture into 1-inch meatballs. In 12-inch skillet brown meatballs in hot oil. Add onion; cook 5 minutes. Drain off fat. Combine cheese soup and the soup can of milk; add to skillet. Cover; simmer 10 minutes. Add beets and sprouts. Cover; simmer 5 minutes. Stir together spinach, biscuit mix, and the ¼ cup milk. Drop spinach mixture atop soup mixture to make eight dumplings. Cover; simmer 10 minutes. Makes 4 servings.

Shaping Meatballs

To shape uniform 1-inch meatballs, try one of these two methods. Form meat mixture into a roll 1 inch in diameter. Cut into 1-inch slices. Round each slice into a ball.

Or, pat meat mixture to a 1-inch-thick square; cut into 1-inch cubes. Round each cube into a ball.

Argentina Stew

Serve the meat and vegetables on a platter—

1 to 1½ pounds beef
    short ribs, cut
    into serving-size
    pieces
5 cups water
2 ounces lean salt
    pork, sliced
    (½ cup)
1½ teaspoons salt
⅛ teaspoon pepper
1 2½- to 3-pound
    broiler-fryer
    chicken, cut up
3 carrots, quartered
3 medium onions,
    quartered
3 tomatoes, quartered

3 medium potatoes,
    peeled and quar-
    tered (1 pound)
½ small head cabbage,
    cut into wedges
6 ounces winter
    squash *or* pump-
    kin, peeled and
    cut into 1-inch
    cubes (1 cup)
1 medium green
    pepper, chopped
    (½ cup)
3 tablespoons snipped
    parsley
1 clove garlic, minced

In 5-quart Dutch oven combine ribs, water, salt pork, salt, and pepper. Bring to boiling. Reduce heat; cover and simmer 1 hour. Add chicken; cover and simmer 25 minutes more. Add carrots, onions, tomatoes, potatoes, cabbage, squash or pumpkin, green pepper, parsley, and garlic; cover and simmer 20 minutes more or till vegetables are tender. Spoon off fat. (*Or,* cool slightly. Refrigerate several hours or overnight. Lift fat from surface. Return mixture to heat. Bring to boiling.) Season to taste with salt and pepper. Remove meat and vegetables from Dutch oven; arrange on platter. Garnish with additional parsley, if desired. Serve with bowls of broth. Makes 6 servings.

Booya

2 cups water
1 tablespoon salt
1 teaspoon dried
    oregano, crushed
1 teaspoon paprika
½ teaspoon dried
    savory, crushed
¼ teaspoon garlic salt
1 cup parsley sprigs
1 pound beef short
    ribs
½ pound boneless
    pork, cut into
    ½-inch cubes
½ pound beef stew
    meat, cut into
    ½-inch cubes
1 28-ounce can toma-
    toes, cut up

1 large onion, sliced
1 cup chopped red
    cabbage
2 medium carrots,
    chopped (1 cup)
1 cup chopped
    rutabaga
2 stalks celery,
    chopped (1 cup)
¼ cup chopped green
    pepper
1 16-ounce can cut
    green beans
1 8½-ounce can peas
1 8-ounce can whole
    kernel corn

In very large kettle or Dutch oven combine water, salt, oregano, paprika, savory, garlic salt, and parsley sprigs. Add ribs, pork, beef, *undrained* tomatoes, onion, cabbage, carrots, rutabaga, celery, and green pepper. Bring to boiling. Reduce heat; cover and simmer about 2 hours or till meat is nearly tender. Remove ribs from soup. When cool enough to handle, remove meat from bones and cube; discard bones. Return meat to kettle; add *undrained* green beans, *undrained* peas, and *undrained* corn. Cover and simmer 30 minutes. Makes 8 to 10 servings.

Crockery cooking directions: Use ingredients as listed above *except* add 2 tablespoons *cooking oil* as follows. In skillet brown ribs, pork, and beef in the 2 tablespoons oil; drain off fat. Place the *undrained* tomatoes, onion, cabbage, carrots, rutabaga, celery, and green pepper in an electric slow crockery cooker.

Place meat atop vegetables. Stir together water, salt, oregano, paprika, savory, garlic salt, and parsley; add to cooker. Cover and cook on low-heat setting for 10 to 12 hours. Remove meat from bones and cube; discard bones. Return meat to cooker; turn to high-heat setting. Add *undrained* beans, *undrained* peas, and *undrained* corn. Cover and cook for 1 hour.

Spanish Beef Soup

1 pound ground beef	1 3-ounce can sliced mushrooms
¾ teaspoon salt	
⅛ teaspoon pepper	¼ cup sliced pimiento-stuffed olives
1 15-ounce can tomato herb sauce	2½ cups water
1 8-ounce can stewed onions, drained	½ cup dry red wine *or* water
2 medium carrots, cut into ½-inch pieces (1 cup)	Grated parmesan cheese (optional)

In large saucepan cook ground beef till browned; drain off fat. Sprinkle meat with salt and pepper. Add tomato herb sauce, onions, carrots, *undrained* mushrooms, and olives. Stir in water and wine. Cover and simmer 30 to 35 minutes or till carrots are tender, stirring occasionally. Sprinkle with parmesan, if desired. Makes 6 servings.

Spicy Hot Chili

1 pound ground beef
   or ground pork
1 medium onion,
   chopped (½ cup)
2 cloves garlic,
   minced
1 16-ounce can toma-
   toes, cut up
1 16-ounce can red
   kidney beans,
   drained
¾ cup tomato juice
1 4-ounce can green
   chili peppers,
   rinsed, seeded,
   and chopped

1 tablespoon worces-
   tershire sauce
2 teaspoons paprika
1 teaspoon sugar
1 teaspoon salt
1 teaspoon dried
   oregano, crushed
½ teaspoon ground
   cumin
¼ teaspoon celery salt
¼ teaspoon cayenne
¼ teaspoon pepper
⅛ teaspoon dry
   mustard
Few drops bottled
   hot pepper sauce

In large saucepan cook meat, onion, and garlic till meat is browned; drain off fat. Stir in *undrained* tomatoes, beans, tomato juice, chili peppers, worcestershire, paprika, sugar, salt, oregano, cumin, celery salt, cayenne, pepper, mustard, hot pepper sauce, and 1 cup *water*. Cover and simmer for 20 to 30 minutes. Makes 4 to 6 servings.

Crockery cooking directions: (Use a 3½-quart or smaller electric slow crockery cooker due to the small volume of chili.) Use ingredients as listed above. In skillet cook meat, onion, and garlic till meat is browned; drain off fat. Transfer meat mixture to electric slow crockery cooker. Stir in remaining ingredients, and ½ cup *water*. Cover and cook on low-heat setting for 8 to 10 hours.

Beef Goulash Soup

4 slices bacon
2 medium onions, chopped
2 cloves garlic, minced
1 to 1½ tablespoons paprika
2 teaspoons salt
2 pounds beef stew meat, cut into 1-inch cubes
1 medium tomato, cut up
1 6-ounce can tomato paste
3 medium potatoes, peeled and finely chopped

In Dutch oven cook bacon till crisp. Drain, reserving drippings; crumble bacon. Cook onions and garlic in reserved drippings till tender. Stir in paprika and salt. Add meat cubes and bacon; cook and stir 2 to 3 minutes. Add tomato, tomato paste, and 2 cups *water*. Cover and simmer 1¼ hours or till meat is nearly tender. Add potatoes. Simmer 20 minutes. Spoon off fat. Serves 6.

Hamburger Soup

1 pound ground beef
1 16-ounce can tomatoes, cut up
2 medium onions, chopped
2 medium carrots, sliced
2 stalks celery, chopped
⅓ cup pearl barley
¼ cup catsup
1 tablespoon instant beef bouillon granules
2 teaspoons seasoned salt
1 teaspoon dried basil, crushed
1 bay leaf

In large saucepan cook ground beef till browned. Drain off fat. Stir in remaining ingredients and 5 cups *water*. Bring to boiling. Reduce heat; cover and simmer for 1 hour. Season to taste with salt and pepper. Remove bay leaf. Serves 6.

Beef and Beer-Vegetable Soup

1 pound ground beef
1 medium onion, chopped (½ cup)
1 12-ounce can beer
1 10½-ounce can *condensed* beef broth
1 soup can water (1¼ cups)
3 medium carrots, thinly sliced (1½ cups)
1 medium turnip, chopped (about 1 cup)

1 stalk celery, thinly sliced (½ cup)
1 4-ounce can mushroom stems and pieces
1 bay leaf
1 teaspoon salt
⅛ teaspoon pepper
⅛ teaspoon ground allspice

In large saucepan cook ground beef and onion till meat is browned; drain off fat. Stir in beer, condensed beef broth, water, carrots, turnip, celery, *undrained* mushrooms, bay leaf, salt, pepper, and allspice. Bring to boiling. Reduce heat; cover and simmer for 30 to 35 minutes or till vegetables are tender. Remove bay leaf. Makes 4 to 6 servings.

Crockery cooking directions: Use ingredients as listed above. In skillet brown meat and onion; drain off fat. Transfer meat and onion to electric slow crockery cooker. Stir in beer, condensed beef broth, water, carrots, turnip, celery, *undrained* mushrooms, bay leaf, salt, pepper, and allspice. Cover and cook on low-heat setting for 8 to 10 hours or till vegetables are tender. Remove bay leaf.

POULTRY

Deviled Chicken Soup

1 3-pound broiler-
  fryer chicken,
  cut up
1 medium onion,
  chopped (½ cup)
1 stalk celery,
  chopped (½ cup)
1 teaspoon salt
¼ teaspoon pepper
1 18-ounce can (2¼
  cups) tomato
  juice
1 16-ounce can cream-
  style corn

1 large potato, peeled
  and chopped
  (1½ cups)
2 tablespoons pre-
  pared mustard
1 teaspoon worcester-
  shire sauce
½ teaspoon chili
  powder
⅛ teaspoon garlic
  powder
  Dash cayenne

In a large kettle combine chicken pieces, onion, celery, salt, and pepper. Add 3 cups *water;* bring to boiling. Reduce heat; cover and simmer about 1 hour or till chicken is tender. Remove chicken from broth. Skim fat from broth. When chicken is cool enough to handle, remove the skin and bones from chicken; discard skin and bones. Cube chicken; set aside.

Stir tomato juice, corn, potato, mustard, worcestershire sauce, chili powder, garlic powder, and cayenne into the broth. Bring to boiling. Reduce heat; cover and simmer for 15 to 20 minutes or till potatoes are nearly tender. Stir in the cubed chicken. Cover and simmer about 5 minutes or till heated through. Season to taste with salt and pepper. Makes 6 servings.

Crockery cooking directions: Use ingredients as listed above. If desired, discard fat and skin from chicken pieces. Combine all ingredients in electric slow crockery cooker. Add 2½ cups *water.* Cover and cook on low-heat setting for 8 hours. Remove chicken with a slotted spoon. Skim fat from broth. When chicken is cool enough to handle, remove skin and bones from chicken; discard skin and bones. Cube chicken; return to soup. Heat through. Season to taste with salt and pepper.

Brunswick Stew

1 2½- to 3-pound broiler-fryer chicken, cut up	1 16-ounce can cream-style corn
6 cups water	1 10-ounce package frozen cut okra
1½ teaspoons salt	1 10-ounce package frozen lima beans
1 teaspoon dried rosemary, crushed	1 large onion, chopped (1 cup)
1 bay leaf	1 tablespoon sugar
2 medium potatoes, peeled and diced (2 cups)	1½ teaspoons salt
1 16-ounce can tomatoes, cut up	½ teaspoon pepper

Place chicken in 5-quart Dutch oven. Add water, 1½ teaspoons salt, rosemary, and bay leaf. Bring to boiling. Reduce heat; cover and simmer about 1 hour or till chicken is tender. Remove chicken from broth. Skim fat from broth. When chicken is cool enough to handle, remove skin and bones from chicken; discard skin and bones. Cut up chicken. Return cut-up chicken to broth. Stir in potatoes, *undrained* tomatoes, corn, okra, beans, onion, sugar, 1½ teaspoons salt, and pepper. Cover and simmer 40 minutes. Remove bay leaf. Makes 8 to 10 servings.

Meaty Basque Vegetable Soup

1 cup dry navy beans
7 cups water
1 2½- to 3-pound
  broiler-fryer
  chicken, cut up
1½ teaspoons salt
12 ounces Polish
  sausage, sliced
2 leeks, sliced
2 medium carrots,
  sliced (1 cup)
1 cup coarsely
  shredded cabbage
1 medium potato,

peeled and cubed
  (1 cup)
1 medium turnip,
  peeled and cubed
  (1 cup)
1 medium onion,
  chopped (½ cup)
1 clove garlic, minced
1 tablespoon snipped
  parsley
1 teaspoon dried
  thyme, crushed
Croutons (optional)

Rinse beans. In Dutch oven or large saucepan, place beans and the water. Bring to boiling; cook 2 minutes. Remove from heat; cover and let stand 1 hour. (Or, combine beans and water; soak overnight.) *Do not drain.* Add chicken pieces and salt. Bring to boiling. Reduce heat; cover and simmer 1 hour.

Remove chicken from bean mixture. When chicken is cool enough to handle, remove skin and bones from chicken; discard skin and bones. Cut up chicken; stir into bean mixture. Stir in Polish sausage, leeks, carrots, cabbage, potato, turnip, onion, garlic, parsley, and thyme. Simmer 30 minutes more or till vegetables are tender. Ladle into bowls; sprinkle with croutons, if desired. Makes 8 servings.

Chicken-Vegetable Stew with Dumplings

2 2½- to 3-pound
    broiler-fryer
    chickens, cut up
4 cups water
3 stalks celery,
    chopped (1½
    cups)
3 medium carrots,
    chopped (1½
    cups)
3 medium onions,
    chopped (1½
    cups)
1 tablespoon salt
1½ teaspoons dried
    thyme, crushed

¼ teaspoon pepper
1 cup cold water
½ cup all-purpose
    flour
1 10-ounce package
    frozen peas
1 4-ounce can mush-
    room stems and
    pieces
Herb Dumplings
    (see recipe, page
    182)
2 tablespoons snipped
    parsley

In Dutch oven or kettle place chicken pieces. Add the
4 cups water, celery, carrots, onions, salt, thyme, and
pepper. Bring to boiling. Reduce heat; cover and simmer for 35 to 45 minutes or till chicken is nearly tender. Skim off fat.

Blend the 1 cup cold water and the flour; stir into
chicken mixture. Stir in frozen peas and *undrained*
mushrooms. Cook, stirring gently, till thickened and
bubbly. Drop Herb Dumpling dough from tablespoon
to make 8 mounds atop bubbling stew. Cover and simmer 15 minutes (do not lift cover). Sprinkle chicken
and dumplings with the snipped parsley. Makes 8
servings.

Broccoli-Chicken Stew

12 chicken thighs,
    skinned (about
    3 pounds)
2 tablespoons cooking
    oil
1 0.6-ounce envelope
    Italian salad
    dressing mix
1 teaspoon salt
3 cups water
½ cup dry white wine
½ cup catsup
• • •
3 medium potatoes,
    peeled and cubed
    (3 cups)

2 cups frozen small
    whole onions
    (½ of a 20-ounce
    package)
1 10-ounce package
    frozen cut
    broccoli
1 medium green
    pepper, cut into
    cubes
2 cups sliced fresh
    mushrooms
    (5 ounces)
⅓ cup cold water
3 tablespoons all-
    purpose flour

In 4½-quart Dutch oven slowly brown chicken thighs,
half at a time, in the hot oil. Remove chicken; drain
fat from pan. In same Dutch oven combine dry salad
dressing mix and salt. Stir in the 3 cups water, wine,
and catsup. Return the browned chicken thighs to pan.
Bring to boiling. Reduce heat; cover and simmer for
15 minutes.

Add potatoes and frozen onions. Simmer, covered,
15 minutes longer. Add frozen broccoli, the green pepper, and mushrooms. Cover and simmer 5 to 10 minutes longer or till vegetables are tender. Blend the ⅓
cup cold water and the flour; stir into stew. Cook and
stir till thickened and bubbly. Makes 6 servings.

Chicken Vegetable-Noodle Soup

Tomatoes, corn, zucchini, and homemade noodles make this a company-special chicken soup—

6 cups water
1 5- to 6-pound stewing chicken, cut up
⅓ cup chopped onion
2 teaspoons salt
¼ teaspoon pepper
1 bay leaf
1 16-ounce can tomatoes, cut up

1 16-ounce can cream-style corn
2 small zucchini, thinly sliced (about 2 cups)
1½ cups uncooked Homemade Noodles (see recipe, page 177)

In a large kettle combine water, chicken pieces, chopped onion, salt, pepper, and bay leaf. Bring to boiling; reduce heat. Cover and simmer about 2 hours or till chicken is tender. Remove chicken from broth. Skim fat from broth; remove bay leaf. When chicken is cool enough to handle, remove skin and bones from chicken; discard skin and bones. Cube chicken; set aside.

Add *undrained* tomatoes, cream-style corn, and thinly sliced zucchini to broth. Bring mixture to boiling. Stir in Homemade Noodles. Cover and simmer about 8 minutes or till noodles are nearly tender. Stir in the cubed chicken. Cover and simmer about 5 minutes more or till heated through. Season to taste with salt and pepper. Makes 8 servings.

QUICK SOUPS

MEAT AND POULTRY

Smoky Beef Chowder

For a change, use thinly sliced ham, pastrami, corned beef, or smoked turkey in this soup—

1 stalk celery, finely
   chopped (½ cup)
1 medium onion,
   finely chopped
   (½ cup)
2 tablespoons butter
   or margarine
3 tablespoons all-
   purpose flour
¼ teaspoon salt
¼ teaspoon dried basil,
   crushed

1 3-ounce package
   thinly sliced
   smoked beef,
   snipped
3 cups milk
¾ cup shredded
   American cheese
   (3 ounces)
1 tablespoon snipped
   parsley

In a medium saucepan cook chopped celery and onion in butter or margarine till onion is tender. Blend in flour, salt, and basil. Stir in smoked beef. Add milk all at once. Cook and stir till thickened and bubbly. Stir in the shredded cheese till melted. Stir in parsley; heat through. Garnish with additional snipped parsley, if desired. Makes 3 or 4 servings.

Reuben Chowder

3 cups milk
1 10¾-ounce can
condensed cream
of celery soup
½ cup shredded
process Swiss
cheese (2 ounces)
1 16-ounce can
sauerkraut,
drained and
snipped
• • •

3 tablespoons butter
or margarine,
softened
4 to 6 slices rye bread
1 teaspoon caraway
seed
• • •
1 12-ounce can corned
beef, chilled and
diced

In a saucepan stir milk into the celery soup and shredded cheese. Add snipped sauerkraut; cover and simmer for 15 minutes.

Meanwhile, spread the butter or margarine over both sides of the rye bread; sprinkle both sides with caraway seed. Cut bread slices into triangles; place on baking sheet. Toast in 300° oven for 20 minutes.

Add diced corned beef to soup. Heat about 10 minutes or till heated through. Serve toast triangles with soup. Makes 4 to 6 servings.

Beefy Bean Soup

3 cups coarsely chopped cabbage
1 medium onion, chopped (½ cup)
2 cups water
1 17-ounce can lima beans
1 11½-ounce can condensed bean with bacon soup
1 tablespoon prepared mustard
1 12-ounce can corned beef, chilled and diced

In saucepan simmer cabbage and onion in the water, covered, for 8 to 10 minutes or till tender. Stir in the *undrained* beans, soup, and mustard. Stir in corned beef; heat through. Serves 4 to 6.

Ham and Pea Soup

2 11¼-ounce cans condensed green pea soup
1 cup chicken broth (see tip, page 174)
2 cups milk
1 6¾-ounce can chunk-style ham, drained and diced, *or* 1 cup diced fully cooked ham
1 2-ounce can mushroom stems and pieces
¼ cup dry white wine

In saucepan combine pea soup and chicken broth; stir in milk. Cook and stir till heated through. Stir in ham, *undrained* mushrooms, and wine; heat through. Serves 4 to 6.

Sausage-Vegetable Chowder

This hearty chowder is made with lima beans—

2 tablespoons butter
or margarine
3 tablespoons all-
purpose flour
1 teaspoon salt
1 teaspoon onion
powder
¼ teaspoon dried
dillweed
⅛ teaspoon pepper
4 cups milk

1 10-ounce package
frozen vegetable,
partially thawed
(lima beans,
cauliflower, green
beans, peas and
carrots, *or*
broccoli)
1 16-ounce can whole
kernel corn,
drained
1 12-ounce package
smoked sausage
links, sliced

In a large saucepan melt butter or margarine over low
heat. Blend in flour, salt, onion powder, dillweed, and
pepper. Add milk all at once. Cook over medium heat,
stirring constantly, till thickened and bubbly.

Cut the partially thawed frozen vegetable into bite-
size pieces, if necessary. Stir the vegetable, corn, and
sausage into the soup. Cover and simmer for 10 to 15
minutes or till vegetable is done. Makes 6 servings.

Quick and Spicy Sausage Chili

1 8-ounce package
   brown-and-serve
   sausage links *or*
   brown-and-serve
   sausage patties,
   cut up
1 small onion,
   chopped (¼ cup)
½ green pepper,
   chopped (¼ cup)
1 8-ounce can pork
   and beans in
   tomato sauce

1 8-ounce can
   tomatoes, cut up
¼ cup water
1 tablespoon chili
   sauce
1 teaspoon chili
   powder
½ teaspoon sugar
¼ teaspoon salt

In a 2-quart saucepan cook sausage, onion, and green pepper till meat is brown and vegetables are tender. Drain off fat.

Stir in the *undrained* pork and beans, *undrained* tomatoes, water, chili sauce, chili powder, sugar, and salt. Bring mixture to boiling. Reduce heat; cover and simmer for 15 to 20 minutes. Makes 2 or 3 servings.

Bratwurst-Potato Chowder

1 4⅝- or 5½-ounce
  package dry
  scalloped potato
  mix
3 cups water
1 10-ounce package
  frozen mixed
  vegetables
3½ cups milk

1 12-ounce package
  fully cooked
  smoked brat-
  wurst, sliced, *or*
1 12-ounce can
  luncheon meat,
  cubed
½ cup milk
2 tablespoons all-
  purpose flour

In a Dutch oven or large saucepan combine the potatoes from the scalloped potato mix with the water. Bring to boiling. Reduce heat; cover and simmer for 5 minutes. Add the frozen mixed vegetables. Return to boiling. Reduce heat; cover and simmer for 10 minutes or till potatoes are tender, stirring occasionally. Stir in the 3½ cups milk and the bratwurst or luncheon meat.

Combine the ½ cup milk, the flour, and the seasoning packet from the scalloped potato mix. Stir into the mixture in saucepan. Cook and stir till thickened and bubbly. Cook 2 minutes longer. Makes 6 to 8 servings.

Tomato-Frankfurter Soup

This soup is perfect for the lunch box. Just store it in a widemouthed vacuum container and with it, pack some fresh fruit—

1 large onion, chopped (1 cup)

8 ounces frankfurters, diagonally sliced (4 or 5)

3 tablespoons butter *or* margarine

• • •

1 11½-ounce can condensed bean with bacon soup

1 10¾-ounce can condensed tomato soup

1½ soup cans water (2 cups)

½ teaspoon sugar

½ teaspoon chili powder

In a medium saucepan cook the chopped onion and sliced frankfurters in the butter or margarine till onion is tender but not brown. Stir in bean with bacon soup, tomato soup, water, sugar, and chili powder. Bring to boiling. Reduce heat; cover and simmer for 5 minutes. Makes 3 or 4 servings.

Orange Chicken Stew

Cook the noodles while the vegetables and seasonings simmer—

2 tablespoons butter *or* margarine

2 tablespoons all-purpose flour

1 8-ounce can tomato sauce

¼ teaspoon finely shredded orange peel

⅓ cup orange juice

⅓ cup water

1 8-ounce can sliced carrots

1 green pepper, cut into ¾-inch squares (about 1 cup)

1 tablespoon minced dried onion

½ teaspoon sugar

¼ teaspoon salt

¼ teaspoon garlic salt

⅛ teaspoon ground allspice

2 5-ounce cans boned chicken, drained and cut up

Hot cooked noodles

In a medium saucepan melt butter or margarine over low heat. Blend in flour. Add tomato sauce, orange peel, orange juice, and water. Cook and stir over medium heat till thickened and bubbly. Stir in *undrained* carrots, green pepper, onion, sugar, salt, garlic salt, and allspice. Bring to boiling. Reduce heat; cover and simmer about 15 minutes. Stir in chicken; heat through. Serve over hot cooked noodles. Makes 3 or 4 servings.

Quick Brunswick Stew

1 large onion, cut in
   thin wedges
1 tablespoon cooking
   oil
1 16-ounce can stewed
   tomatoes, cut up
1 16-ounce can sliced
   potatoes, drained
   and cut up
1 12-ounce can whole
   kernel corn

1 10¾-ounce can
   condensed tomato
   soup
1 8-ounce can lima
   beans, drained
½ teaspoon salt
   Dash pepper
2 5-ounce cans boned
   chicken, drained
   and cut up

In a large saucepan cook onion wedges in cooking oil
till tender but not brown; stir in *undrained* stewed
tomatoes, sliced potatoes, *undrained* whole kernel corn,
tomato soup, lima beans, salt, and pepper. Bring mixture to boiling. Reduce heat; cover and simmer mixture
for 10 minutes. Carefully stir in the cut-up chicken;
continue cooking till heated through. Makes 6 servings.

Peanut-Chicken Soup

¼ cup all-purpose
  flour
2 teaspoons paprika
1 2½- to 3-pound
  broiler-fryer
  chicken, cut up
3 tablespoons cooking
  oil
1 large green pepper,
  chopped (¾ cup)
1 medium onion,
  chopped (½ cup)
3 cups water
3 medium tomatoes,

finely chopped
  (1½ cups)
2 teaspoons salt
⅛ teaspoon cayenne
¾ cup creamy peanut
  butter
2 cups sliced fresh
  okra or 1 10-ounce
  package frozen
  whole okra, sliced
1 4½-ounce can
  medium shrimp,
  drained and
  deveined

Combine flour and paprika. Coat chicken pieces with
flour mixture, using all of the mixture. In large saucepan or Dutch oven brown chicken slowly in hot cooking oil over medium heat about 15 minutes, turning to
brown evenly. Remove chicken and set aside. Cook
green pepper and onion in pan drippings till tender
but not brown. Spoon off excess fat. Add water, tomatoes, salt, cayenne, and chicken pieces to pan. Bring
to boiling. Reduce heat; cover and simmer 20 minutes.

In small saucepan heat peanut butter over low heat
till melted; gradually blend in about *1 cup* of the hot
broth from chicken mixture. Return all to chicken mixture. Stir in okra and shrimp; return to boiling. Reduce
heat; cover and simmer 20 minutes or till chicken is
tender. Serves 4 to 6.

Chicken-Zucchini Stew

Sample this sophisticated, yet inexpensive, chicken entrée—

1½ teaspoons salt
½ teaspoon pepper
¼ teaspoon paprika
1 2½- to 3-pound broiler-fryer chicken, cut up
2 tablespoons cooking oil
2 cups chicken broth (see tip, page 174)
3 medium potatoes, peeled and quartered

1 medium onion, chopped (½ cup)
½ teaspoon dried sage, crushed
• • •
3 medium zucchini, sliced (3 cups)
1 4-ounce can mushroom stems and pieces, drained
¼ cup dry white wine
3 tablespoons all-purpose flour

Combine salt, pepper, and paprika. Rub mixture onto chicken pieces. In large saucepan or Dutch oven brown chicken in hot cooking oil over medium heat about 15 minutes, turning to brown evenly. Add broth, potatoes, onion, and sage. Cover and simmer for 25 minutes.

Stir in zucchini and mushrooms. Simmer about 10 minutes more or till vegetables are tender. Remove chicken and vegetables to serving dish; cover and keep warm.

Blend wine and flour; stir into the broth mixture. Cook and stir till thickened and bubbly. Spoon sauce over chicken and vegetables in serving dish. Makes 4 servings.

Chicken Cider Stew

2 cups apple cider *or* juice
3 tablespoons catsup
2 slices bacon, cut up
1½ teaspoons salt
¼ teaspoon dried savory, crushed
¼ teaspoon dried basil, crushed
⅛ teaspoon pepper
1 2- to 2½-pound broiler-fryer chicken *or* rabbit, cut up

4 carrots, thinly sliced
2 medium sweet potatoes, peeled and quartered
2 medium onions, finely chopped (1 cup)
1 stalk celery, cut into 1-inch pieces
1 apple, peeled, cored, and chopped (1 cup)
3 tablespoons all-purpose flour

In large kettle or Dutch oven stir together first seven ingredients. Add chicken or rabbit. Bring to boiling. Reduce heat; cover and simmer for 45 minutes. Stir in carrots, sweet potatoes, onions, celery, and apple. Cover and simmer about 30 minutes or till meat and vegetables are tender. Blend the flour and ¼ cup cold *water*; stir into hot stew. Cook and stir till mixture is thickened and bubbly. Makes 4 servings.

Crockery cooking directions: Use ingredients as listed above. Place carrots, sweet potatoes, onions, celery, and apple in electric slow crockery cooker. Add chicken or rabbit. Combine *1½ cups* of the apple cider, the catsup, bacon, salt, savory, basil, and pepper. Pour over meat and vegetables. Cover and cook on low-heat setting for 10 to 12 hours. Turn cooker to high-heat setting. Blend the flour with the remaining ½ cup cider; stir into hot stew. Cover and cook 15 minutes or till thickened and bubbly.

SAUSAGE

Beef and Sausage Stew

Beef stew with the added flavor of bacon, Polish sausage, cabbage, and apple—

4 slices bacon
1 pound beef stew
    meat, cut into
    1-inch cubes
3 medium apples,
    peeled, cored,
    and chopped
    (2¾ cups)
1 large onion,
    chopped (1 cup)
3½ cups beef broth
    (see tip, page 174)

1 teaspoon salt
    • • •
1 pound Polish
    sausage links, cut
    into bite-size
    pieces
6 medium carrots,
    sliced (3 cups)
6 cups chopped
    cabbage
¼ cup all-purpose
    flour

In 4½-quart Dutch oven cook bacon till crisp. Drain, reserving drippings in pan. Crumble bacon and set aside. Brown stew meat in the reserved drippings. Add apples and onion. Cover and simmer for 5 minutes. Add 3 *cups* of the beef broth to pot; stir in salt. Bring to boiling. Reduce heat; cover and simmer about 1¼ hours or till meat is nearly tender.

Stir in sausage pieces and carrots. Cover and simmer for 30 minutes. Stir in cabbage; cover and simmer 10 minutes more. Blend the remaining ½ cup beef broth and flour. Stir into stew. Cook and stir till thickened and bubbly. Top each serving with some crumbled bacon. Makes 8 servings.

Sausage Soup

            2 slices bacon
            1 pound bulk pork sausage
            1 medium onion, sliced
         3½ cups beef broth (see tip, page 174)
            1 8-ounce can *each* French-style green beans, cut
               wax beans, *and* butter beans, drained
            ½ teaspoon worcestershire sauce
            ⅛ teaspoon dry mustard

In skillet cook bacon till crisp. Drain, reserving drippings. Crumble bacon; set aside. Cook sausage and onion in bacon drippings till meat is brown and onion is tender. Remove sausage and onion from skillet; drain on paper toweling. In saucepan combine sausage, onion, broth, the 3 kinds of drained beans, worcestershire, mustard, ¼ teaspoon *salt*, and dash *pepper*. Heat through, stirring occasionally. Top each serving with bacon. Serves 4.

Dutch Pea Soup

            1 pound bulk pork sausage
            1 pound dry split peas
            7 cups water
            2 fresh pigs' feet (1¼ pounds)
            1 cup finely chopped onion
            1 large potato, peeled and shredded (1 cup)
            2 teaspoons salt

Shape sausage into ¾-inch balls; brown on all sides in Dutch oven. Drain, reserving 2 tablespoons fat in pan. Rinse peas; add to pan. Stir in remaining ingredients. Bring to boiling; cover and simmer for 1½ hours. Remove pigs' feet; cut off any meat and return to soup. Discard bones. Heat soup; season to taste. Makes 8 to 10 servings.

Chorizo-Garbanzo Stew

If you like, you can freeze part of this Mexican-style stew to serve another time—

1 pound dry garbanzo
beans (2½ cups)
13 cups water
1 pound beef shank
crosscuts
1 pound smoked pork
hocks (ham
hocks)
1 large onion,
chopped (1 cup)
2 teaspoons salt

2 teaspoons paprika
1 pound chorizo *or*
Italian sausage
links, sliced
2 medium potatoes,
peeled and diced
(2 cups)
4 slices bacon, crisp-
cooked, drained,
and crumbled

Rinse beans. In 10-quart kettle or Dutch oven combine beans and the water. Bring to boiling; reduce heat and simmer 2 minutes. Remove from heat. Cover; let stand 1 hour. (Or, soak beans in the water overnight in a covered pan.) *Do not drain.*

Add beef shank crosscuts, smoked pork hocks, chopped onion, salt, and paprika. Cover and simmer for 2 hours or till beans are tender. Remove meats. Skim fat from soup. When meats have cooled slightly, remove meat from bones and dice. Discard bones.

Return meat to soup. Stir in sausage pieces and potatoes. Bring to boiling. Reduce heat; cover and simmer 20 minutes longer or till potatoes are tender. Sprinkle each serving with some crumbled bacon. Makes 16 servings.

Oven Potato Sausage-Lentil Stew

8 ounces dry lentils (1¼ cups)	2 tablespoons butter *or* margarine
1½ pounds potato sausage *or* Polish sausage, cut into ½-inch pieces	2 tablespoons all-purpose flour
2 medium carrots, chopped (1 cup)	1 cup water
3 cups water	½ cup dry red wine
• • •	2 teaspoons instant chicken bouillon granules
1 stalk celery, chopped (½ cup)	¾ teaspoon dried thyme, crushed
1 medium onion, chopped (½ cup)	¾ teaspoon salt
	⅛ teaspoon pepper

Rinse lentils; in saucepan combine with potato sausage or Polish sausage, and carrots. Add the 3 cups water; bring to boiling. Reduce heat; cover and simmer for 30 minutes.

In skillet cook chopped celery and onion in butter or margarine till tender but not brown. Blend in flour; stir in the 1 cup water, the wine, chicken bouillon granules, thyme, salt, and pepper. Bring to boiling, stirring constantly.

In a 2½-quart casserole combine the lentil-sausage mixture with the wine mixture. Bake, uncovered, in 375° oven for 40 minutes, stirring once or twice. Makes 6 servings.

German Sausage Chowder

1 pound fully cooked smoked bratwurst *or* knackwurst links, cut into ½-inch pieces (8 links)
2 medium potatoes, peeled and chopped (2 cups)
1 medium onion, chopped (½ cup)
1½ teaspoons salt
Dash pepper
2 cups water
1 small head cabbage, shredded (4 cups)
3 cups milk
3 tablespoons all-purpose flour
1 cup shredded Swiss cheese (4 ounces)
Snipped parsley

In large saucepan or Dutch oven combine sausage,
potatoes, onion, salt, and pepper. Add water. Bring to
boiling. Reduce heat; cover and simmer 20 minutes or
till potatoes are nearly tender. Stir in cabbage; cook
10 minutes more or till vegetables are tender. Stir in
2½ *cups* of the milk. Blend remaining ½ cup milk and
flour; stir into soup. Cook and stir till thickened and
bubbly. Stir in cheese till melted. Garnish with parsley. Makes 6 servings.

Sausage Substitutions

Vary the flavor of a soup by using a different
sausage with similar qualities. Try Italian sausage or chorizo instead of bulk pork sausage.
Or, substitute beerwurst, Polish sausage, or
smoked bratwurst for frankfurters. And when
a recipe calls for pepperoni, experiment with
hard salami or summer sausage.

Beerwurst Soup

2 stalks celery, chopped (1 cup)

1 medium onion, chopped (½ cup)

2 tablespoons butter *or* margarine

1 tablespoon cornstarch

½ teaspoon dry mustard

¼ teaspoon dried oregano, crushed

¼ teaspoon dried basil, crushed

¼ teaspoon dried thyme, crushed

¼ teaspoon garlic powder

1 13¾-ounce can (1¾ cups) beef broth

1 12-ounce can (1½ cups) beer

¾ pound beerwurst (beer salami), thinly sliced and quartered

• • •

4 slices French bread cut 1 inch thick

1 cup shredded mozzarella cheese (4 ounces)

In large skillet cook the chopped celery and onion in butter or margarine till tender but not brown. Blend in cornstarch, dry mustard, oregano, basil, thyme, and garlic powder. Add beef broth and beer. Cook and stir till thickened and bubbly. Cover and simmer over low heat for 30 minutes, stirring occasionally. Add beerwurst; simmer 2 to 3 minutes to heat through.

Place bread slices on baking sheet; sprinkle with the shredded mozzarella cheese. Broil 3 inches from heat for 3 minutes or till cheese is melted and lightly browned. Ladle soup into 4 bowls; top each with a bread slice. Makes 4 servings.

VEAL, VENISON, AND LAMB

Veal-Mushroom Oven-Style Burgoo

Burgoo is another name for a meat and vegetable stew.

2 pounds boneless
   veal, cut into
   1-inch cubes
2 tablespoons cooking
   oil
¼ cup all-purpose
   flour
2 tablespoons pre-
   pared mustard
2 teaspoons instant
   beef bouillon
   granules
1½ teaspoons salt

1 teaspoon sugar
1 18-ounce can (2¼
   cups) tomato
   juice
1 cup water
6 small carrots
12 whole pearl onions
   or frozen small
   whole onions
2 cups sliced fresh
   mushrooms (5
   ounces)

In large skillet brown meat, *half* at a time, in hot oil. Remove meat to a 3-quart casserole, leaving meat juices in skillet. Stir flour, mustard, bouillon granules, salt, and sugar into meat juices in skillet. Add tomato juice and water; cook and stir till thickened and bubbly. Pour over meat in casserole. Cover and bake in 350° oven for 1 hour.

Cut carrots in half crosswise and then into quarters lengthwise to form thin sticks. Stir carrots, onions, and mushrooms into stew. Cover and bake for 45 to 60 minutes more or till meat and vegetables are tender. Stir before serving. Makes 6 servings.

French Veal Stew

¼ cup all-purpose
flour
1 teaspoon salt
¼ teaspoon pepper
2 pounds boneless
veal, cut into
¾-inch cubes
¼ cup cooking oil
6 medium carrots, cut
into ½-inch
pieces
1 large onion, quar-
tered
1 stalk celery, halved
3 sprigs parsley
2 cloves garlic,
minced

1 bay leaf
½ teaspoon salt
½ teaspoon dried
thyme, crushed
½ teaspoon dried
basil, crushed
2 cups water
½ cup dry sherry
• • •
3 egg yolks
1 tablespoon lemon
juice
1 tablespoon milk
Hot cooked noodles
(optional)

In paper or plastic bag combine flour, the 1 teaspoon
salt, and the pepper. Add veal cubes, a few at a time,
shaking to coat. In large skillet brown veal cubes, *half*
at a time, in hot oil. Return all veal to skillet. Add carrots, onion, celery, parsley, garlic, bay leaf, the ½ teaspoon salt, thyme, and basil. Stir in water and sherry.
Bring to boiling. Reduce heat; cover and simmer about
1 hour or till meat is tender. Discard celery, parsley,
and bay leaf.

In a bowl beat together egg yolks, lemon juice, and
milk. Stir about *1 cup* of the hot mixture into egg yolk
mixture; return to remaining hot mixture, stirring constantly. Heat through, stirring constantly. Serve over
noodles, if desired. Makes 6 to 8 servings.

Blanquette de Veau

3 cups sliced fresh
mushrooms,
(8 ounces)
2 tablespoons butter
or margarine
3 pounds boneless
veal, cut into
1-inch cubes
2 cloves garlic,
minced
1 pound small whole
onions (about 16)
1 cup light cream

⅓ cup all-purpose
flour
1 teaspoon instant
chicken bouillon
granules
1 teaspoon salt
⅛ teaspoon white
pepper
¼ cup dry sherry
¼ cup snipped parsley
Hot cooked noodles
(optional)

In large skillet cook mushrooms in butter or margarine
till tender. Remove mushrooms to a 3-quart casserole.
In same skillet over medium-low heat, cook veal and
garlic, covered, for 15 minutes, stirring frequently. Do
not allow meat to brown.

Meanwhile, cook onions in boiling salted water for
10 minutes; drain. Add meat and onions to casserole.
Measure pan juices; add enough water to make 1 cup
liquid. Return liquid to skillet. Blend together light
cream and flour. Add to pan juices. Stir in bouillon
granules, salt, and pepper. Cook and stir till mixture is
thickened and bubbly. Pour over meat and onions in
casserole.

Bake in 350° oven about 1 hour or till meat is tender.
Stir in sherry. Sprinkle with parsley. Serve with hot
cooked noodles, if desired. Makes 8 to 10 servings.

Venison Stew

1 pound boneless venison *or* beef stew meat cut into ½-inch cubes

1½ cups water

1 teaspoon salt

⅛ teaspoon coarsely ground pepper

½ cup dry red wine

4 medium carrots, cut into thirds

2 medium potatoes, peeled and cubed (2 cups)

1 cup fresh *or* frozen cranberries

1 medium onion, chopped (½ cup)

1 stalk celery, cut into julienne strips

1 clove garlic, minced

2 tablespoons sugar

2 tablespoons worcestershire sauce

1½ teaspoons Hungarian *or* regular paprika

3 juniper berries (optional)

2 whole cloves

1 bay leaf

½ cup cold water

¼ cup rye flour

Cooked wild rice *or* sliced French bread

In 3-quart saucepan combine venison or beef stew meat with the 1½ cups water, salt, and pepper. Bring to boiling. Reduce heat; cover and simmer 1¼ hours. Stir in wine, carrots, potatoes, cranberries, onion, celery, garlic, sugar, worcestershire sauce, paprika, juniper berries, cloves, and bay leaf. Cover and simmer for 45 minutes or till vegetables are tender. Combine the ½ cup cold water and rye flour; stir into stew. Cook and stir till thickened and bubbly. Remove bay leaf. Serve stew with wild rice or sliced French bread. Makes 4 servings.

Irish Stew

1 pound boneless
   lamb, cut into
   1-inch cubes
1 medium onion, cut
   into thin wedges
1 bay leaf
1½ teaspoons salt
¼ teaspoon pepper
   • • •
2 medium potatoes,
   peeled and thinly
   sliced (2 cups)

1 medium turnip,
   peeled and
   chopped (1 cup)
1 9-ounce package
   frozen cut green
   beans
1 tablespoon snipped
   parsley
¼ teaspoon dried
   basil, crushed
¼ teaspoon dried
   oregano, crushed

In large saucepan or Dutch oven combine lamb, onion, bay leaf, salt, and pepper. Add 4 cups *water*. Bring to boiling. Reduce heat; cover and simmer for 1 hour. Stir in potatoes, turnip, green beans, parsley, basil, and oregano. Cover and cook 25 to 30 minutes more or till vegetables are tender. Remove bay leaf. Season to taste. Makes 6 servings.

Crockery cooking directions: Use ingredients as listed above. In electric slow crockery cooker combine onion, bay leaf, salt, pepper, potatoes, turnip, green beans, parsley, basil, and oregano. Add lamb cubes; pour 2½ cups *water* over all. Cover and cook on low-heat setting for 10 to 12 hours. Remove bay leaf. Season to taste.

Lamb Paprikash

2 pounds lean bone-
less lamb, cut into
1-inch pieces
2 tablespoons cooking
oil
1 clove garlic,
minced
1 16-ounce can toma-
toes, cut up
1 large onion,
chopped (1 cup)

2 teaspoons salt
1 to 2 teaspoons
paprika
½ cup cold water
3 tablespoons all-
purpose flour
1 cup dairy sour
cream
Hot cooked noodles
Snipped parsley

In large skillet brown *half* the lamb in hot oil; set
aside. Brown remaining lamb and garlic; return all to
skillet. Stir in *undrained* tomatoes, onion, salt, and
paprika. Bring to boiling. Reduce heat; cover and simmer 1 to 1½ hours or till meat is tender. Blend water
and flour; stir into stew. Cook and stir till thickened
and bubbly. Stir about ½ *cup* of the hot gravy into
sour cream. Return to stew. Heat through but *do not
boil.* Serve over hot noodles. Sprinkle with parsley.
Makes 6 servings.

Crockery cooking directions: Use ingredients as
listed above *except* omit the cooking oil. In electric
slow crockery cooker combine lamb, garlic, *undrained*
tomatoes, onion, salt, and paprika. Cover and cook on
low-heat setting 8 to 10 hours.

Turn cooker to high-heat setting; spoon off any fat.
Blend cold water and flour; stir into meat mixture.
Cover; cook 20 to 30 minutes or till thickened and
bubbly. Stir mixture occasionally. Blend about ½ *cup*
of the hot mixture into sour cream; return to stew in
cooker. Heat through. Serve over hot cooked noodles;
sprinkle with parsley.

LAMB, PORK, AND HAM

Dilled Lamb Ragout

Garnish stew with lemon wedges and fresh dill—

2 pounds boneless lamb, cut into ¾-inch cubes
⅓ cup all-purpose flour
½ teaspoon dried dillweed
¼ cup cooking oil
1 10-ounce package (2 cups) frozen peas
1 cup sliced celery
½ cup rosé wine
1 cup dairy sour cream.

Coat lamb with mixture of flour, dillweed, 1½ teaspoons *salt*, and dash *pepper*. In Dutch oven brown lamb, *half* at a time, in hot oil. Return all meat to pan. Stir in any remaining flour mixture. Blend in 2 cups *water*. Bake, covered, in 375° oven 45 minutes. Stir in peas, celery, and wine; cover and bake 45 minutes more. Skim off fat. Stir in sour cream. Heat through but *do not boil*. Serves 6.

Ham Hodgepodge

5 cups chopped cabbage
6 large carrots, cut into 1-inch pieces (1 pound)
2 large potatoes, peeled and chopped (3 cups)
2 cups diced fully cooked ham (10 ounces)
½ cup chopped onion
½ teaspoon seasoned salt
1 15-ounce can garbanzo beans

In Dutch oven combine first six ingredients. Cover; simmer 1 hour. Add *undrained* beans; cover and cook 10 to 15 minutes. (Add more water, if needed.) Makes 6 to 8 servings.

Lamb and Lentil Soup

This meaty soup made with lamb shanks, a ham hock, and knackwurst tastes like a French cassoulet—

4 lamb shanks (about 3 pounds)
1 medium smoked pork hock (ham hock)
1 medium onion, chopped (½ cup)
1 clove garlic, halved
1½ teaspoons salt
¼ teaspoon pepper
8 cups water

• • •

1½ cups dry lentils

2 knackwurst links, sliced (about 6 ounces)
2 medium carrots, chopped (1 cup)
1 cup dry red wine
3 tablespoons snipped parsley
½ teaspoon dried thyme, crushed
¼ teaspoon dried rosemary, crushed

In very large kettle combine lamb shanks, pork hock, onion, garlic, salt, and pepper. Add the water; bring to boiling. Reduce heat; cover and simmer for 2 hours.

Remove lamb shanks and pork hock. When meats are cool enough to handle, cut off meat and chop. Return chopped meat to broth; discard bones.

Rinse lentils; add to soup. Stir in sliced knackwurst, carrots, wine, parsley, thyme, and rosemary. Cover and simmer mixture 45 to 50 minutes or till lentils and carrots are tender. Skim off fat. Season to taste with salt and pepper. Makes 8 servings.

Ham-Spinach Chowder

1 10-ounce package
   frozen chopped
   spinach
½ cup chopped onion
1 10¾-ounce can
   condensed cream
   of potato soup
3½ cups milk
3 cups cubed fully
   cooked ham
   (1 pound)

¼ cup snipped parsley
2 teaspoons prepared
   mustard
¾ teaspoon salt
½ teaspoon dried
   basil, crushed
Dash pepper
3 tablespoons all-
   purpose flour

In large saucepan cook frozen spinach and onion according to spinach package directions; drain well. Blend potato soup into spinach. Stir in 3 *cups* of the milk, the ham, parsley, mustard, salt, basil, and pepper. Cook over low heat till heated through; stir occasionally.

Blend the remaining ½ cup milk and the flour; stir into ham mixture. Cook and stir till thickened and bubbly. If desired, dot each serving with butter or margarine. Serves 6.

Microwave cooking directions: In 2-quart nonmetal casserole place frozen spinach and onion. Cook, covered with waxed paper, in counter-top microwave oven on high power for 5 to 7 minutes or till vegetables are tender, stirring and breaking up spinach once. Drain. Blend potato soup into spinach mixture.

Stir in 3 *cups* of the milk, the ham, parsley, mustard, salt, basil, and pepper. Micro-cook, covered, about 5 minutes or till heated through, stirring once. Blend the remaining ½ cup milk and flour; stir into ham mixture. Micro-cook, uncovered, for 8 to 10 minutes or till slightly thickened and bubbly, stirring every 2 minutes. Serve as above.

Hot and Hearty Ham Soup

Cheese-topped rye bread slices float atop individual servings of soup—

1 1½- to 1¾-pound
    meaty ham bone
    or 1½ pounds
    smoked pork
    hocks (ham
    hocks)
8 cups water
8 whole black pepper-
    corns
5 whole cloves
1 teaspoon salt
1 clove garlic, halved
3½ cups coarsely
    chopped cabbage

2 large potatoes,
    peeled and thinly
    sliced (3 cups)
3 large carrots, thinly
    sliced (2 cups)
1 medium onion,
    chopped (½ cup)
6 to 8 thick slices rye
    bread
¼ cup grated parme-
    san cheese
4 ounces Swiss cheese,
    cut into strips

In 4½-quart Dutch oven combine ham bone or hocks, water, peppercorns, cloves, salt, and garlic; bring to boiling. Reduce heat; cover and simmer 2½ hours. Remove ham bone; when bone is cool enough to handle, cut off meat and chop. Discard bone. Strain broth. Return broth and meat to Dutch oven. Add cabbage, potatoes, carrots, and onion. Cover and simmer 40 minutes or till vegetables are tender. Season to taste with salt and pepper.

Meanwhile, toast bread. Ladle soup into heat-proof bowls. Top each with a toast slice; sprinkle with parmesan and top with Swiss cheese. Place under broiler 2 minutes or till cheese melts. (Or, if you don't have heat-proof bowls, place toast slices on baking sheet; top with cheese, and broil. Float atop soup servings.) Makes 6 to 8 servings.

Broccoli and Ham Soup

2 cups diced fully cooked ham (10 ounces)
1 medium onion, chopped (½ cup)
1 clove garlic, minced
2 tablespoons butter *or* margarine
2 10¾-ounce cans *condensed* chicken broth
2 cups chopped fresh broccoli *or* 1 10-ounce package frozen chopped broccoli
1½ cups water
1 8-ounce can tomatoes, cut up
½ cup elbow macaroni
¼ teaspoon ground nutmeg
Grated parmesan cheese (optional)

In 3-quart saucepan cook ham, onion, and garlic in butter or margarine till onion is tender. Stir in condensed chicken broth, fresh or frozen chopped broccoli, water, *undrained* tomatoes, uncooked macaroni, and nutmeg. Bring to boiling. Reduce heat; cover and simmer for 8 to 10 minutes or till broccoli and macaroni are tender. Season to taste with some salt and pepper. Sprinkle individual servings with parmesan cheese, if desired. Makes 6 servings.

Cutting Tomatoes

When a recipe calls for cut-up canned tomatoes, do the cutting in the can. Insert a sharp knife into the open can and cut tomatoes against the side of the can. Or, use kitchen shears to snip the tomatoes. Draining is usually unnecessary, since you'll also use the liquid.

Schnitz Und Knepp

If you buy home-style dried apples you'll need to add them earlier—

- 1 2- to 2½-pound smoked pork shoulder roll
- 4 cups chicken broth (see tip, page 174)
- 2 cups water
- 8 ounces dried apples (2 cups)
- 2 tablespoons brown sugar
  Potato Dumplings *or* Fluffy Dumplings (see recipe, page 179)

Trim excess fat from pork. Place pork in 4½-quart Dutch oven; add broth and water. Bring to boiling; cover and simmer 1½ to 2 hours or till pork is tender. Turn meat occasionally during cooking. Skim fat from broth. Remove meat; cut into bite-size pieces. Return meat to Dutch oven. Add apples and sugar. Bring to boiling, stirring to dissolve sugar.

Prepare Potato or Fluffy Dumplings. Drop dough from tablespoon into 8 mounds atop bubbling broth. Cover tightly and let mixture return to boiling. Reduce heat (don't lift cover); simmer 30 minutes for Potato Dumplings or 15 minutes for Fluffy Dumplings. (Potato Dumplings will be soft.) To serve, remove dumplings to serving bowl with slotted spoon; pour meat and apple mixture around dumplings. Makes 8 servings.

Potato Dumplings: In saucepan barely cover 4 medium *potatoes* (1¼ pounds) with water. Add 1 teaspoon *salt.* Bring to boiling. Reduce heat; cover and simmer for 20 minutes or till potatoes are tender. Drain and cool slightly. Peel potatoes. Mash with 2 tablespoons *butter or margarine* and ½ teaspoon *salt* till very smooth. Stir in ¼ cup all-purpose *flour* and 2 beaten *eggs;* mix well.

Sweet-Sour Pork Stew

Use fresh or frozen pea pods to make this stew—

¼ cup all-purpose
    flour
1 teaspoon salt
    Dash pepper
2 pounds boneless
    pork, cut into
    ¾-inch cubes
2 tablespoons cooking
    oil
1½ cups chicken broth
    (see tip, page 174)
⅓ cup catsup
2 tablespoons vinegar
1 tablespoon brown
    sugar

1 teaspoon salt
1 teaspoon worcester-
    shire sauce
1 large onion,
    chopped (1 cup)
4 cups fresh pea pods
    or 2 6-ounce pack-
    ages frozen pea
    pods partially
    thawed
    Hot cooked rice *or*
    hot cooked
    noodles

In paper or plastic bag combine flour, 1 teaspoon salt, and the pepper. Add pork cubes, a few at a time, shaking to coat. In large saucepan or Dutch oven brown meat, *half* at a time, in hot oil. Return all meat to saucepan.

Combine chicken broth, catsup, vinegar, brown sugar, 1 teaspoon salt, and worcestershire sauce. Stir into meat; add onion. Cover and simmer about 1 hour or till meat is tender, stirring occasionally. Stir in fresh or frozen pea pods; cover and simmer 3 to 5 minutes longer or till pea pods are crisp-tender. Serve with rice or noodles. Makes 6 to 8 servings.

Pork Brunswick Stew

Serve with seasoned croutons for added flavor and texture—

¾ cup soft bread
   crumbs (1 slice)
¼ cup milk
¾ teaspoon salt
¾ teaspoon ground
   sage
1 pound ground pork
2 tablespoons cooking
   oil
1 28-ounce can toma-
   toes, cut up

1 16-ounce can whole
   kernel corn
1 medium onion,
   chopped (½ cup)
1 tablespoon vinegar
1 tablespoon prepared
   mustard
2 teaspoons sugar
1½ teaspoons salt
½ teaspoon worcester-
   shire sauce

Combine crumbs, milk, the ¾ teaspoon salt, and sage.
Add pork; mix well. Shape into 36 one-inch balls. In
Dutch oven brown meatballs, *half* at a time, in hot oil.
Drain off fat. Return all meatballs to Dutch oven; stir
in remaining ingredients. Bring to boiling. Reduce
heat; cover and simmer 30 minutes. Makes 4 to 6
servings.

Microwave cooking directions: Use ingredients as
listed above *except* omit cooking oil. Mix and shape
meatballs as directed above.

Arrange meatballs in a 12x7½x2-inch nonmetal baking dish. Cook, covered with waxed paper, in countertop microwave oven on high power about 6 minutes or
till meat is done; rearrange twice. Drain and set aside.

In 3-quart nonmetal casserole combine remaining
ingredients, omitting oil. Micro-cook, covered, 11 to
12 minutes or till heated through, stirring twice. Stir
in meatballs. Micro-cook, uncovered, 1 minute more.

Pork and Cabbage Soup

This meal-in-a-dish soup combines shredded cabbage and pork cubes in a beef-tomato broth—

1 pound lean boneless pork, cut into ½-inch cubes

1 tablespoon cooking oil

1 10¾-ounce can condensed tomato soup

1 10½-ounce can *condensed* beef broth

2 soup cans water (2½ cups)

1 small head cabbage, shredded (4 cups)

1 medium onion, chopped (½ cup)

¼ cup dry sherry

1 bay leaf

1 teaspoon salt

½ teaspoon paprika

Dash pepper

• • •

Dairy sour cream

In 4½-quart Dutch oven brown pork cubes in hot cooking oil. Drain off excess fat. Stir in tomato soup, condensed beef broth, water, shredded cabbage, chopped onion, sherry, bay leaf, salt, paprika, and pepper. Bring mixture to boiling. Reduce heat; cover and simmer 40 minutes or till meat is tender. Remove bay leaf. Season to taste with additional salt and pepper. Top each serving with a dollop of sour cream. Garnish with a parsley sprig, if desired. Makes 5 or 6 servings.

South American Pork Soup

This soup can be made in an electric slow crockery cooker or a Dutch oven—

1½ pounds lean boneless pork *or* beef, cut into ½-inch cubes

2 tablespoons cooking oil

1 medium onion, finely chopped (½ cup)

1 clove garlic, minced

1 teaspoon paprika

2 medium potatoes, peeled and cut into ½-inch cubes (2 cups)

2 medium sweet potatoes, peeled and cut into ½-inch cubes (2 cups)

2 medium carrots, chopped (1 cup)

½ small winter squash, peeled and cut into ½-inch cubes (1 cup)

1 8-ounce can whole kernel corn

1 tomato, peeled and chopped

2 teaspoons salt

¼ teaspoon pepper

2 cups torn fresh spinach

In 4-quart Dutch oven or kettle brown *half* the meat in hot oil; remove from pan. Brown remaining meat with onion, garlic, and paprika. Return all meat to pan. Add 3 cups *water*. Bring to boiling. Reduce heat; cover and simmer 1¼ hours. Add potatoes, sweet potatoes, carrots, squash, *undrained* corn, tomato, salt, and pepper. Cover; simmer 15 to 20 minutes more or till meat and vegetables are tender. Stir in spinach; simmer 3 to 5 minutes more. Season to taste with salt and pepper. Makes 8 servings.

Crockery cooking directions: Use ingredients as listed above. In large skillet brown *half* the meat in hot oil; set aside. Brown remaining meat with onion, garlic, and paprika. In electric slow crockery cooker arrange potatoes, sweet potatoes, carrots, squash, *undrained* corn, tomato, salt, and pepper. Place meat and onion mixture atop vegetables; pour 2½ cups *water* over all. Cover and cook on low-heat setting for 8

hours or till meat and vegetables are tender. Turn to
high-heat setting. Stir in spinach. Cover and cook 10
minutes or till spinach is slightly wilted. Season to
taste.

Fresh Cauliflower-Ham Chowder

This creamy chowder is also easy to make—

2 medium potatoes,
  peeled and cubed
  (2 cups)
1 cup water
1 medium onion,
  chopped (½ cup)
1 tablespoon instant
  chicken bouillon
  granules
2 cups sliced cauli-
  flowerets

3 cups milk
2½ cups cubed fully
  cooked ham
⅛ teaspoon ground
  nutmeg
⅛ teaspoon white
  pepper
2 tablespoons all-
  purpose flour
Snipped parsley

In a large saucepan simmer potatoes, water, onion,
and bouillon granules, covered, for 10 minutes. Add
cauliflower and cook about 10 minutes more or till
tender. Stir in 2½ *cups* of the milk, the ham, nutmeg,
and pepper. Bring to boiling. Blend remaining ½ cup
milk with flour. Stir into hot mixture. Cook and stir till
thickened and bubbly. Garnish with snipped parsley.
Makes 4 to 6 servings.

Barbecue Pork Stew

2 pounds boneless
pork, cut into
1-inch cubes
1 to 2 tablespoons
cooking oil
1 clove garlic, minced
3 cups water
1 teaspoon salt
¼ teaspoon pepper

• • •

1 small head cabbage,
coarsely chopped
(4 cups)
1 15-ounce can tomato
sauce
1 cup whole pearl
onions *or* frozen

small whole
onions
1 medium green
pepper, chopped
(½ cup)
½ cup dry red wine
2 tablespoons brown
sugar
2 tablespoons pre-
pared mustard
½ teaspoon ground
ginger
¼ teaspoon cayenne
Corn Dumplings
(see recipe, page
181)

In Dutch oven brown *half* the pork in hot oil. Remove
from pan. Brown remaining pork and garlic. Drain off
fat. Return all meat to Dutch oven. Add water, salt,
and pepper. Bring to boiling. Reduce heat; cover and
simmer for 30 minutes. Stir in cabbage, tomato sauce,
onions, green pepper, wine, brown sugar, mustard,
ginger, and cayenne. Cover and simmer 20 minutes
longer or till meat and vegetables are nearly tender.
Drop dumplings atop boiling mixture. Cover and simmer 10 to 12 minutes longer or till dumplings are done.
Makes 8 servings.

FISH AND SEAFOOD

Seafood Gumbo

½ cup all-purpose
   flour
½ cup cooking oil
2 medium onions,
   finely chopped
   (1 cup)
2 stalks celery, finely
   chopped (1 cup)
1 medium green
   pepper, finely
   chopped (½ cup)
2 cloves garlic,
   minced
8 cups water
1½ teaspoons salt

½ teaspoon bottled
   hot pepper sauce
1 pound fresh or
   frozen crab meat,
   thawed
1 pound fresh or
   frozen shelled
   shrimp
1 pint shucked oysters
¼ cup sliced green
   onion tops
¼ cup snipped parsley
1 tablespoon filé
   powder (optional)
Hot cooked rice

In Dutch oven or kettle blend together flour and oil.
Cook over medium heat 15 minutes or till mixture is a
dark reddish-brown color. Stir frequently for the first
10 minutes and stir constantly for the last 5 minutes.
Add onions, celery, green pepper, and garlic. Cook and
stir about 8 minutes or till vegetables are lightly
browned. Add water, salt, and hot pepper sauce. Bring
to boiling. Reduce heat; cover and simmer 1 hour.

Add crab meat and shrimp; simmer, uncovered, 15
minutes more. Add oysters and oyster liquid; simmer
about 5 minutes more or just till edges of oysters curl.
Stir in green onion tops and parsley. Blend a small
amount of the hot liquid into filé powder; return all to
kettle. Season to taste with salt and pepper. Ladle into
bowls over mounds of rice. Makes 8 to 10 servings.

Whiting Stew

2 pounds fresh *or* frozen dressed whiting *or* other fish	2 tablespoons olive *or* cooking oil
2 cups water	2 medium potatoes, peeled and sliced
⅓ cup snipped parsley	2 large carrots, sliced (1 cup)
4 cloves garlic	3 tomatoes, peeled and cubed
½ teaspoon salt	1 teaspoon salt
1 medium onion, sliced	¼ teaspoon pepper
1 stalk celery, sliced (½ cup)	

Thaw fish, if frozen. Remove skin from fish. In 10-inch skillet combine fish, water, parsley, garlic, and the ½ teaspoon salt. Bring mixture to boiling. Reduce heat; cover and simmer gently about 2 to 3 minutes or till fish flakes easily when tested with a fork.

In 4-quart Dutch oven cook onion and celery in hot oil till vegetables are tender but not brown. Add potatoes and carrots; cook and stir till lightly browned. Stir in tomatoes, the 1 teaspoon salt, and the pepper.

Strain stock from fish; discard parsley and garlic. Add stock to Dutch oven. Bring to boiling. Reduce heat, cover pan tightly and simmer about 30 minutes or till vegetables are tender.

Meanwhile remove and discard bones from fish; break fish into chunks. Add fish to vegetable mixture; heat through. Makes 6 servings.

Seafood Stew

1 6-ounce package
 frozen crab meat
1 pound fresh *or*
 frozen fish fillets
8 clams in shells
2 cups Fish Stock (see
 recipe, page 175)
1 16-ounce can toma-
 toes, cut up
¾ cup dry white wine
1 ear fresh corn, cut
 into 1-inch pieces
 or 1 8-ounce can
 whole kernel
 corn, drained

½ cup chopped green
 pepper
1 medium onion,
 chopped (½ cup)
2 tablespoons snipped
 parsley
1 bay leaf
1 clove garlic, minced
1 teaspoon salt
1 teaspoon dried
 thyme, crushed
¼ teaspoon thread
 saffron, crushed
¼ teaspoon pepper

Partially thaw crab meat and fish. Remove skin from
fish fillets; cut fillets into 1-inch pieces. Thoroughly
wash clams. Cover clams with salted water using 3
tablespoons salt to 8 cups cold water. Let stand 15
minutes; rinse. Repeat twice.

In large saucepan combine Fish Stock, *undrained*
tomatoes, wine, corn, green pepper, onion, parsley,
bay leaf, garlic, salt, thyme, saffron, and pepper. Bring
to boiling. Reduce heat; cover and simmer for 30 minutes. Add crab, fish, and clams. Cook 4 to 5 minutes
or till fish flakes easily with a fork and clams open.
Do not overcook. Discard bay leaf. Serve stew with
French bread slices, if desired. Makes 6 to 8 servings.

Scallop-Wine Soup

    1 pound fresh *or* frozen scallops, thawed
    1 large onion
    2 tablespoons butter
    ¼ cup all-purpose flour
 3½ cups milk
    1 4-ounce can mushroom stems and pieces, drained
    ½ cup dry white wine
    ½ cup shredded Swiss cheese
    1 tablespoon snipped parsley

Halve large scallops. Cut onion into thin wedges. Cook onion in butter, covered, over low heat 15 minutes or till tender; stir occasionally. Stir in flour. Add milk; cook and stir over medium-high heat till bubbly. Add mushrooms, scallops, 1 teaspoon *salt,* and dash *pepper.* Cover; simmer 5 minutes. Stir in wine; heat. Top with cheese and parsley. Serves 6.

Shrimp Bisque

    1 cup chopped celery
    1 cup diced potato
    ½ cup chopped onion
    2 cups milk
    2 tablespoons all-purpose flour
    1 8-ounce package frozen precooked shrimp,
        thawed
    2 tablespoons butter

In saucepan combine celery, potato, onion, 1 cup *water,* ½ teaspoon *salt,* and dash *pepper.* Bring to boiling. Reduce heat; cover and simmer 15 minutes or till potatoes are tender, stirring occasionally. Blend milk and flour; stir into potato mixture. Add shrimp and butter. Cook and stir till thickened and bubbly. Garnish with snipped parsley, if desired. Makes 4 servings.

Fish Soup

This soup is adapted from a Chilean favorite, Caldillo de Pescado—

1½ pounds fresh *or* frozen fish fillets
1 large onion, chopped (1 cup)
1 clove garlic, minced
2 tablespoons olive *or* cooking oil
2 cups water
2 small potatoes, peeled and diced (1½ cups)

2 tomatoes, peeled and diced (1 cup)
½ cup dry white wine
½ teaspoon salt
Dash pepper
2 beaten egg yolks
2 tablespoons snipped parsley

Thaw fish, if frozen; cut fish into ¾-inch pieces. In large saucepan cook and stir the chopped onion and garlic in hot olive or cooking oil till onion is tender but not brown. Stir in water, potatoes, tomatoes, wine, salt, and pepper. Bring to boiling. Reduce heat; cover and simmer 20 minutes. Add fish pieces; return to boiling. Cover and simmer 10 minutes or till fish flakes easily when tested with a fork.

Gradually stir about *1 cup* of the hot liquid into the beaten egg yolks; return all to saucepan. Cook and stir gently till mixture is slightly thickened and bubbly. Stir in the snipped parsley. Makes 6 to 8 servings.

Fish-Wine Chowder

1 pound fresh *or*
  frozen brook trout
  or pike fillets
1 pound fresh *or*
  frozen halibut *or*
  haddock fillets
6 slices bacon
1 medium onion,
  chopped (½ cup)
2 shallots, chopped
  (1 tablespoon)
1½ cups white bur-
  gundy *or* aligote
1½ cups water

1 teaspoon salt
¼ teaspoon dried
  thyme, crushed
1 stalk celery, quar-
  tered
2 cloves garlic, halved
4 sprigs parsley
2 whole cloves
3 tablespoons all-
  purpose flour
3 tablespoons butter
  or margarine,
  softened
¼ cup light cream

Thaw fish, if frozen; cut fish into bite-size pieces. Cook bacon in 4½-quart Dutch oven; drain, reserving 2 tablespoons drippings. Crumble bacon and set aside. Cook onion and shallots in reserved bacon drippings till tender. Remove from heat. Add wine, water, salt, and thyme. Tie celery, garlic, parsley, and whole cloves in cheesecloth to make a *bouquet garni;* add to pan. Bring to boiling. Reduce heat; cover and simmer for 20 minutes. Remove cheesecloth bag. Add fish to Dutch oven. Cover and cook gently about 8 to 10 minutes or till fish flakes when tested with a fork.

Blend flour and softened butter or margarine to a smooth paste; stir into simmering liquid. Stir in cream. Cook and stir till thickened and bubbly. Return bacon to pan. Season to taste. Makes 8 servings.

Fish Goulash

2 medium onions,
sliced
1 medium green pepper, cut into rings
2 cloves garlic,
minced
3 tablespoons butter
or margarine
1 tablespoon paprika
1 15-ounce can tomato
sauce
2 cups water

2 teaspoons sugar
1½ teaspoons salt
½ teaspoon dried marjoram, crushed
1½ pounds fresh or frozen haddock, halibut, or salmon steaks, cut ¾ inch thick
10 cherry tomatoes,
halved

Thaw fish, if frozen. Cut steaks into 6 serving-size pieces. In 5-quart Dutch oven cook onions, green pepper, and garlic in butter or margarine about 10 minutes or till the vegetables are tender but not brown. Stir in paprika; cook and stir over low heat 2 to 3 minutes. Stir in tomato sauce, water, sugar, salt, and marjoram. Add fish. Bring to boiling. Reduce heat; simmer, uncovered, 15 minutes or till fish flakes easily with a fork. Add tomatoes; cook 5 minutes more. Remove fish to bowls; spoon soup atop. Makes 6 servings.

Fish Terms

A dressed fish is one that's been eviscerated and scaled.

Steaks are crosscut slices from a large, dressed fish. They contain a cross section of the backbone.

Fillets are pieces cut lengthwise from the sides and away from the backbone. They're generally boneless pieces.

Bouillabaisse Gumbo

1 16-ounce can stewed
  tomatoes
1 10¾-ounce can
  condensed
  tomato soup
1 10¾-ounce can
  condensed
  chicken gumbo
  soup
2 soup cans water
  (2½ cups)
1 medium sweet
  potato, peeled
  and chopped
  (1 cup)
1 stalk celery,
  chopped (½ cup)

⅓ cup chopped green
  onion
1 tablespoon snipped
  parsley
1 tablespoon worces-
  tershire sauce
1 clove garlic, minced
2 dashes bottled hot
  pepper sauce
1 bay leaf
1 7½-ounce can
  minced clams
1 4½-ounce can
  shrimp, drained
  and deveined
Salt and pepper

In large saucepan combine *undrained* stewed tomatoes, condensed tomato soup, condensed chicken
gumbo soup, water, sweet potato, celery, green onion,
parsley, worcestershire sauce, garlic, bottled hot pepper sauce, and bay leaf. Bring mixture to boiling. Reduce heat; cover and simmer about 30 minutes or till
vegetables are tender. Add *undrained* clams and
drained shrimp. Simmer about 10 minutes or till mixture is heated through. Season to taste with salt and
pepper. Remove bay leaf before serving. Makes 6 to 8
servings.

Monterey Fish Stew

1 pound fresh *or*
  frozen firm, white
  fish (such as cod,
  haddock, or sole)
1 small onion, diced
  (⅓ cup)
1 clove garlic, minced
2 tablespoons butter
  or margarine
1 cup water
⅓ cup dry vermouth
2 teaspoons instant
  chicken bouillon
  granules
¾ teaspoon salt
½ teaspoon dried mar-
  joram, crushed
⅛ teaspoon pepper

1 bay leaf
2 potatoes, peeled
  and sliced
  (2 cups)
1 carrot, sliced
  (½ cup)
2 medium tomatoes,
  peeled and
  chopped (1½
  cups)
5 or 6 fresh mush-
  rooms, quartered
2 tablespoons snipped
  parsley
¼ cup cold water
2 tablespoons corn-
  starch

Thaw fish, if frozen; cut fish into bite-size pieces. In
3-quart saucepan cook onion and garlic in butter or
margarine till tender but not brown. Stir in the 1 cup
water, the vermouth, bouillon granules, salt, marjoram,
pepper, and bay leaf. Add potatoes and carrot; bring
to boiling. Reduce heat; cover and simmer about 20
minutes or till vegetables are just tender. Add fish,
tomatoes, mushrooms, and parsley. Cover and simmer
about 5 minutes or till fish flakes easily with a fork.

Remove fish and vegetables; set aside. Blend the ¼
cup cold water and cornstarch; stir into pan. Cook and
stir till thickened and bubbly. Return fish and vegetables to sauce; heat through. Serves 4.

Tuna-Cheese Chowder

A terrific family-style soup—

2 medium carrots, shredded (1 cup)
1 medium onion, chopped (½ cup)
¼ cup butter *or* margarine
¼ cup all-purpose flour
2 cups milk
2 cups chicken broth (see tip, page 174)
1 6½- or 7-ounce can tuna, drained and flaked
½ teaspoon celery seed
½ teaspoon worcestershire sauce
¼ teaspoon salt
1 cup shredded American cheese (4 ounces)
Snipped chives

In 3-quart saucepan cook carrots and onion in butter or margarine till onion is tender but not brown. Blend in flour. Add milk and chicken broth. Cook and stir till thickened and bubbly. Stir in tuna, celery seed, worcestershire sauce, and salt. Heat through. Add cheese; heat and stir till cheese is melted. Garnish with snipped chives. Makes 4 servings.

Testing Fish for Doneness

The test for doneness of fish is simple. Place fork tines into fish at a 45-degree angle and twist the fork. If the fish flakes apart easily and is milky white, it is done just right. If it resists flaking and still has some translucency, the fish needs additional cooking.

Eggplant-Zucchini Fish Stew

This fish stew is chock-full of interesting vegetables—

2 pounds fresh *or*
    frozen fish fillets
1 medium onion,
    thinly sliced
1 large green pepper,
    chopped (¾ cup)
1 clove garlic, minced
2 tablespoons cooking
    oil
3 cups tomato juice
1½ teaspoons salt
1 teaspoon sugar

1 teaspoon dried
    basil, crushed
¼ teaspoon pepper
1 medium eggplant,
    peeled and diced
    (5 cups)
2 medium zucchini,
    sliced (about
    2 cups)
Grated parmesan
    cheese

Thaw fish, if frozen. Remove skin from fillets and cut fillets into 1-inch pieces; set aside. In 4-quart Dutch oven cook onion, green pepper, and garlic in hot oil till onion is tender but not brown. Stir in tomato juice, salt, sugar, basil, and pepper. Add eggplant; cover and cook about 10 minutes or till eggplant is tender. Stir in zucchini and fish. Cover and cook 10 to 15 minutes longer or till zucchini is tender and fish flakes easily when tested with a fork; stir occasionally. Ladle into soup bowls and sprinkle each serving with some grated parmesan cheese. Serves 6 to 8.

Skip Jack Chowder

1 cup chopped red onion	Dash bottled hot pepper sauce
¼ cup snipped parsley	1 pint shucked oysters
2 tablespoons butter	2 cups milk
1 tablespoon soy sauce	½ cup light cream
1 teaspoon dried thyme, crushed	2 cups shredded American cheese (8 ounces)
½ teaspoon salt	½ cup dry white wine
1 bay leaf	

In saucepan cook onion and parsley in butter till onion is tender. Stir in soy, thyme, salt, bay leaf, and pepper sauce. Add *undrained* oysters; cook and stir over medium heat 5 minutes or till edges of oysters curl. Stir in milk and cream; heat through. Stir in cheese till melted. Remove from heat; stir in wine. Remove bay leaf. Makes 6 servings.

Oyster Stew

1 pint shucked oysters
¾ teaspoon salt
2 cups milk
1 cup light cream
  Dash bottled hot pepper sauce (optional)
  Paprika
  Butter *or* margarine

In a medium saucepan combine *undrained* oysters and salt. Cook over medium heat about 5 minutes or till edges of oysters curl. Stir in milk, cream, and hot pepper sauce. Heat through. Season to taste with salt and pepper. Sprinkle each serving with paprika and top with a pat of butter. Makes 4 servings.

Cioppino

1 pound fresh *or*
frozen fish fillets

½ large green pepper,
cut into ½-inch
squares

2 tablespoons finely
chopped onion

1 clove garlic, minced

1 tablespoon cooking
oil

1 16-ounce can toma-
toes, cut up

1 8-ounce can tomato
sauce

½ cup dry white *or*
red wine

3 tablespoons snipped
parsley

½ teaspoon salt

¼ teaspoon dried
oregano, crushed

¼ teaspoon dried
basil, crushed

Dash pepper

2 4½-ounce cans
shrimp, drained
and deveined, *or*
1 12-ounce pack-
age frozen shelled
shrimp

1 7½-ounce can
minced clams

Thaw fish, if frozen. Remove skin from fillets and cut
fillets into 1-inch pieces; set aside.

In 3-quart saucepan cook green pepper, onion, and
garlic in oil till onion is tender but not brown. Add
undrained tomatoes, tomato sauce, wine, parsley, salt,
oregano, basil, and pepper. Bring to boiling. Reduce
heat; cover and simmer 20 minutes.

Add fish pieces, shrimp, and *undrained* clams to tomato mixture. Bring just to boiling. Reduce heat; cover
and simmer 5 to 7 minutes or till fish and shrimp are
done. Makes 6 servings.

Bouillabaisse

1 pound small fresh
   or frozen lobster
   tails
1 pound fresh *or*
   frozen red snap-
   per *or* sole fillets
1 pound fresh *or*
   frozen cod *or*
   haddock fillets
12 ounces fresh *or*
   frozen scallops
12 clams in shells
2 large onions,
   chopped (2 cups)
⅓ cup olive *or* cooking
   oil

6 cups Fish Stock
   (see recipe, page
   175) *or* water
1 28-ounce can toma-
   toes, cut up
2 small cloves garlic,
   minced
2 sprigs parsley
2 bay leaves
1 tablespoon salt
1½ teaspoons dried
   thyme, crushed
½ teaspoon thread
   saffron, crushed
⅛ teaspoon pepper
   French bread slices

Thaw shellfish and fish, if frozen. When lobster is partially thawed, split tails in half lengthwise; cut crosswise to make 6 to 8 portions. Cut fish fillets into 2-inch
pieces. Cut large scallops in half. Wash clams well. Set
seafood aside.

In large saucepan or Dutch oven cook onions in hot
oil till tender but not brown. Add Fish Stock, *undrained* tomatoes, garlic, parsley, bay leaves, salt,
thyme, saffron, and pepper. Bring to boiling. Reduce
heat; cover and simmer 30 minutes. Strain stock into
a large kettle; discard vegetables and herbs.

Bring strained stock to boiling; add lobster and fish
and cook 5 minutes. Add scallops and clams; boil 5
minutes or till clams open. Serve in shallow bowls with
French bread. Makes 6 to 8 servings.

Snapper Stew with Lemon Dumplings

1½ pounds fresh *or*
  frozen red snap-
  per *or* other fish
  fillets
  Lemon Dumplings
  (see recipe, page
  180)
  • • •
2 cups Fish Stock
  (see recipe, page
  175)
1 16-ounce can toma-
  toes, cut up
2 medium carrots,
  sliced (1 cup)

2 stalks celery, sliced
  (1 cup)
1 teaspoon salt
½ teaspoon dried
  basil, crushed
  • • •
½ cup cold water
⅓ cup all-purpose
  flour
1 large cucumber,
  finely chopped
  (1 cup)

Thaw fish, if frozen. Remove skin from fillets and cut
fillets into 1-inch pieces. Prepare dough for Lemon
Dumplings; set aside.

In a 4-quart Dutch oven or kettle combine Fish
Stock, *undrained* tomatoes, carrots, celery, salt, and
basil. Bring mixture to boiling. Reduce heat; cover and
simmer for 5 minutes.

In a screw-top jar combine water and flour. Cover
and shake till smooth. Stir flour-water mixture into simmering stock; cook and stir till mixture is thickened
and bubbly. Add the fish pieces to mixture. Return to
boiling and add cucumber. Drop Lemon Dumpling
dough from a tablespoon to make 6 mounds atop boiling soup. Reduce heat; cover and simmer for 20 minutes or till fish and dumplings are done. Makes 6
servings.

QUICK SOUPS

FISH AND SEAFOOD

Spinach-Fish Soup

 2 cups milk
 1 11-ounce can condensed cheddar cheese soup
 1 10-ounce package frozen chopped spinach,
   thawed and well-drained
 1 tablespoon worcestershire sauce
 ½ teaspoon salt
 1 pound frozen fish fillets, thawed and cubed

In a 3-quart saucepan stir together milk, cheese soup, spinach, worcestershire sauce, and salt. Bring to boiling; add fish. Reduce heat; cover and simmer about 10 minutes or till fish is done. Makes 4 servings.

Speedy Clam Chowder

    4 slices bacon
    ¼ cup chopped onion
    1 10¾-ounce can condensed cream of potato soup
    1 7½-ounce can minced clams
    ½ cup milk
       Paprika

In saucepan cook bacon till crisp. Drain, reserving 2
tablespoons drippings in pan. Crumble bacon and set
aside. Cook onion in reserved drippings until tender.
Stir in potato soup, *undrained* clams, and milk. Simmer, uncovered, 5 to 10 minutes; stir occasionally. Stir
in bacon; sprinkle with paprika. Makes 3 servings.

Salmon-Potato Chowder

    2 cups milk
    1 10¾-ounce can condensed cream of potato soup
    ½ of a 10-ounce package (1 cup) frozen peas
    1 16-ounce can salmon, drained, flaked, and skin
       and bones removed
    1 cup shredded American cheese (4 ounces)
    ¼ teaspoon salt
    ⅛ teaspoon pepper

In 3-quart saucepan stir the milk into the cream of
potato soup. Stir in the frozen peas. Bring mixture to
boiling. Reduce heat; cover and simmer for 5 minutes.
Add salmon, shredded cheese, salt, and pepper. Heat,
stirring gently, till cheese melts and soup is heated
through. Makes 4 servings.

Kitchen Shelf Bouillabaisse

1 7½-ounce can crab
   meat
1 16-ounce can
   tomatoes, cut up
1½ cups clam juice
1 6½- or 7-ounce can
   water-pack tuna,
   drained and
   flaked
½ cup dry white wine
1 tablespoon minced
   dried onion
1 teaspoon dried
   parsley flakes

1 teaspoon
   worcestershire
   sauce
¼ teaspoon dried
   thyme, crushed
¼ teaspoon garlic
   powder
5 slices French
   bread, toasted
Grated parmesan
   cheese

Drain crab meat, reserving liquid. Break meat into chunks, discarding any cartilage. In a large saucepan combine the crab, reserved crab liquid, *undrained* tomatoes, clam juice, tuna, white wine, dried onion, parsley flakes, worcestershire sauce, thyme, and garlic powder. Bring mixture to boiling. Reduce heat and simmer, uncovered, for 10 minutes. Ladle into soup bowls; top each serving with a slice of toasted French bread. Pass grated parmesan cheese to sprinkle atop. Makes 5 servings.

Corn and Clam Chowder

Bacon flavors this colorful, easy-to-fix chowder—

4 slices bacon
1 medium onion, chopped (½ cup)
2 tablespoons all-purpose flour
2 cups milk

• • •

1 16-ounce can mixed vegetables, drained

2 7½-ounce cans minced clams
1 8½-ounce can cream-style corn
½ teaspoon salt
¼ teaspoon pepper

In a 3-quart saucepan cook bacon till crisp. Drain, reserving 1 tablespoon drippings in pan. Crumble bacon and set aside.

In the same pan cook onion in reserved bacon drippings till tender but not brown. Stir in the flour. Add the milk all at once; cook and stir till the mixture is thickened and bubbly.

Stir in the mixed vegetables, *undrained* clams, cream-style corn, salt, and pepper. Heat through. Garnish soup with the crumbled bacon. Makes 6 servings.

Quick Fish Chowder

3 slices bacon	1 pound frozen fish fillets, thawed and diced
4 cups frozen fried hash brown potatoes (16 ounces)	3 cups milk
1 cup water	¼ cup snipped parsley
1 medium onion, chopped (½ cup)	1 teaspoon salt
1 10¾-ounce can condensed cream of shrimp soup	¼ teaspoon dried thyme, crushed
	Paprika
	Butter *or* margarine (optional)

In saucepan cook bacon till crisp, drain, reserving drippings in pan. Crumble bacon and set aside. Add frozen hash brown potatoes, water, and chopped onion to bacon drippings in pan; bring to boiling. Reduce heat; cover and simmer about 10 minutes or till vegetables are tender. Blend in cream of shrimp soup. Stir in the diced fish; cook about 15 minutes longer or till fish is done. Stir in milk, snipped parsley, salt, and thyme; heat through.

To serve, sprinkle each serving with some of the crumbled bacon and a little paprika. Top with a pat of butter or margarine, if desired. Makes 6 servings.

Crab Chowder

You'd never believe such an elegant soup is so easy to make—

1 10-ounce package frozen cauliflower
2 cups milk
2 tablespoons sliced green onion
2 tablespoons diced pimiento
½ teaspoon salt
1 cup light cream
3 tablespoons all-purpose flour

1 7½-ounce can crab meat, drained, cartilage removed, and cut up
1 3-ounce package cream cheese, cubed

In 3-quart saucepan cook cauliflower according to package directions; *do not drain*. Cut up any large pieces. Stir in milk, sliced green onion, pimiento, and salt. Heat and stir *just* till boiling.

Combine the light cream and flour; add to hot milk mixture. Cook and stir till thickened and bubbly. Add crab meat and cubed cream cheese; heat and stir till cream cheese melts and soup is heated through. Season to taste with some additional salt and pepper. Makes 4 servings.

VEGETABLES

Vegetarian Chili

Sprinkle individual servings of this meatless chili with cubes of cheese—

1 cup dry pinto beans
4 cups water
1 16-ounce can whole kernel corn
1 15-ounce can tomato sauce
1 large onion, chopped (1 cup)
1 4-ounce can green chili peppers, rinsed, seeded, and chopped

1 tablespoon chili powder
1 teaspoon salt
1 teaspoon dried oregano, crushed
1 clove garlic, minced
1 bay leaf

• • •

2 cups cubed cheddar *or* monterey jack cheese (8 ounces)

Rinse beans. In large saucepan combine beans and the water. Bring to boiling; reduce heat and simmer 2 minutes. Remove from heat. Cover; let stand 1 hour. (Or, soak beans in the water overnight in a covered pan.) *Do not drain.*

In a large saucepan combine pinto beans with liquid, *undrained* corn, tomato sauce, onion, chopped chili peppers, chili powder, salt, oregano, garlic, and bay leaf. Bring to boiling. Reduce heat; cover and simmer for 2 to 2½ hours. Remove bay leaf. Ladle chili into individual serving bowls. Sprinkle each serving with cheddar or monterey jack cheese cubes. Serve immediately. Makes 6 to 8 servings.

Black Bean Soup

1 pound dry black
beans
8 cups water
1 large onion, finely
chopped (1 cup)
2 medium carrots,
finely chopped
(1 cup)
2 cloves garlic,
minced
¼ cup butter *or*
margarine

1 16-ounce can toma-
toes, cut up
2 tablespoons worces-
tershire sauce
2 teaspoons salt
¼ teaspoon pepper
1 bay leaf
2 hard-cooked eggs,
sliced

Rinse beans. In large saucepan combine beans and
water. Bring to boiling; reduce heat and simmer 2
minutes. Remove from heat. Cover; let stand 1 hour.
(Or, soak beans in the water overnight in a covered
pan.) *Do not drain.*

In 4-quart Dutch oven or kettle cook onion, carrots,
and garlic in butter or margarine till onion is tender.
Stir in beans and liquid, *undrained* tomatoes, worcestershire, salt, pepper, and bay leaf. Cover and simmer
2½ to 3 hours or till beans are done. Remove bay leaf.
Mash beans slightly. Top with egg slices. Makes 8 to
10 servings.

Crockery cooking directions: Use ingredients as
listed above. In saucepan combine beans and water.
Bring to boiling; reduce heat and simmer for 1½
hours. Pour beans and liquid into a bowl; cover and
chill.

Drain beans; reserve liquid. In electric slow crockery cooker combine beans with remaining ingredients,
except eggs. Add enough reserved bean liquid to cover
solids (about 2¼ cups). Cover and cook on low-heat
setting 12 to 14 hours. Remove bay leaf. Mash beans
slightly. Top with egg slices.

Ham and Bean Vegetable Soup

1 pound dry navy
beans (2½ cups)
8 cups water
1½ pounds meaty
smoked pork
hocks (ham
hocks)
2 medium potatoes,
peeled and cubed
(2 cups)
2 medium carrots,
chopped (1 cup)

2 stalks celery, sliced
(1 cup)
1 medium onion,
chopped (½ cup)
¾ teaspoon dried
thyme, crushed
½ teaspoon salt
¼ teaspoon pepper
Several dashes
bottled hot
pepper sauce

Rinse beans. In 4-quart Dutch oven combine beans and the water. Bring to boiling; reduce heat and simmer 2 minutes. Remove from heat. Cover; let stand 1 hour. (Or, soak beans in the water overnight in a covered pan.) *Do not drain.*

Bring beans and liquid to boiling. Add smoked pork hocks. Reduce heat; cover and simmer for 1 hour or till beans are nearly tender. Remove pork hocks. When hocks are cool enough to handle, cut off meat and coarsely chop. Discard bones. Return meat to pan. Add potatoes, carrots, celery, onion, thyme, salt, pepper, and hot pepper sauce. Cover and simmer 30 minutes or till vegetables are tender. Season to taste with salt and pepper. Makes 8 to 10 servings.

Country-Style Bean Soup

Pork sausage adds extra flavor to this lima bean soup—

1 pound dry lima
  beans (2½ cups)
8 cups water
1 teaspoon salt
    • • •
8 ounces bulk pork
  sausage
2 medium apples,
  peeled and cubed
  (2 cups)
1 large onion,
  chopped (1 cup)

2 stalks celery,
  chopped (1 cup)
1 clove garlic, minced
1 28-ounce can toma-
  toes, cut up
2 tablespoons brown
  sugar
2 tablespoons pre-
  pared mustard
1 teaspoon salt
¼ teaspoon pepper

Rinse beans. In 5-quart Dutch oven or kettle combine beans and the water. Bring to boiling. Reduce heat; cover and simmer 2 minutes. Remove from heat. Cover; let stand 1 hour. (Or, soak beans in the water overnight in a covered pan.) *Do not drain.* Add 1 teaspoon salt. Bring to boiling. Reduce heat; cover and simmer the beans 1 hour.

In a skillet cook pork sausage with apples, onion, celery, and garlic till sausage is done; spoon off fat. Stir sausage mixture into the beans. Stir in the *undrained* tomatoes, brown sugar, mustard, 1 teaspoon salt, and the pepper. Cover and simmer 1 hour longer. Serve in bowls. Makes 8 to 10 servings.

Vegetable Soup with Basil Pistou

8 ounces dry navy
  beans (1¼ cups)
7 cups water
1 10¾-ounce can
  condensed
  chicken broth
2 teaspoons salt
⅛ teaspoon pepper
1 large onion,
  chopped (1 cup)
½ cup diced salt pork
  (4 ounces)
2 potatoes, peeled
  and diced
2 medium carrots,
  diced
2 small zucchini,
  sliced
2 small tomatoes,
  peeled and
  chopped
1½ cups coarsely
  chopped cabbage

1 cup bias-sliced
  green beans
1 cup fresh shelled
  lima beans *or*
  ½ of a 10-ounce
  package frozen
  lima beans
1 medium turnip,
  peeled and diced
  (1 cup)
½ cup chopped celery
3 cups lightly packed
  fresh basil leaves,
  snipped
1 cup grated gruyère
  cheese (4 ounces)
2 cloves garlic
1 teaspoon lemon
  juice
¼ teaspoon salt
½ cup olive oil

Rinse beans. In 5-quart Dutch oven combine beans, water, broth, the 2 teaspoons salt, and the pepper. Bring to boiling; reduce heat and simmer 2 minutes. Remove from heat. Cover; let stand 1 hour. (Or, add water, broth, salt, and pepper to beans. Cover and refrigerate overnight.) *Do not drain.* Return to boiling; cover and simmer 1½ hours.

In a skillet cook onion and salt pork till pork is brown. Add to beans. Stir in potatoes, carrots, zucchini, tomatoes, cabbage, green beans, lima beans, turnip, and celery. Bring to boiling. Reduce heat; cover and simmer 30 to 40 minutes or till vegetables are just tender.

To make pistou, place basil, gruyère cheese, garlic, lemon juice, and the ¼ teaspoon salt in blender container. Cover and blend till smooth. (Or, place in mortar; pound with pestle to a smooth paste.) Add olive oil, a teaspoon at a time, till the mixture is consistency of soft butter.

To serve, ladle soup into bowls. Pass pistou to stir into each serving. Makes 10 servings.

Potato-Cheese Soup

    3 medium potatoes, peeled and cut up
    1 small onion, finely chopped (⅓ cup)
      Milk
    3 tablespoons butter *or* margarine, melted
    2 tablespoons all-purpose flour
    2 tablespoons snipped parsley
    ¾ teaspoon salt
      Dash pepper
    1 cup shredded Swiss cheese (4 ounces)

In 2-quart saucepan add potatoes and onion to 1 cup lightly salted boiling *water*. Cover and cook about 20 minutes or till potatoes are tender. Mash potatoes slightly; do not drain. Measure mixture and add enough milk to make 5 cups. Blend melted butter, flour, parsley, salt, and pepper. Stir into potato mixture in saucepan; cook and stir till thickened and bubbly. Add cheese; cook and stir till cheese is partially melted. Serve immediately. Makes 4 or 5 servings.

Cheesy Beer-Vegetable Soup

This hearty soup combines parsnips, green pepper, corn, and mushrooms with the flavors of beer and cheese—

1 large onion, finely chopped (1 cup)	1 12-ounce can beer
1 medium green pepper, chopped (½ cup)	1 4-ounce can mushroom stems and pieces
2 tablespoons butter *or* margarine	½ teaspoon dry mustard
2 cups chopped parsnips	⅓ cup cold water
1 16-ounce can whole kernel corn	3 tablespoons all-purpose flour
2 cups chicken broth (see tip, page 174)	2 cups shredded American cheese (8 ounces)

In 3-quart saucepan cook onion and green pepper in butter or margarine till tender but not brown. Add parsnips, *undrained* corn, chicken broth, beer, *undrained* mushrooms, and mustard. Bring to boiling. Reduce heat; cover and simmer 20 to 30 minutes or till parsnips are done.

In screw-top jar combine water and flour. Cover; shake till thoroughly mixed. Stir into hot vegetable mixture. Cook and stir till slightly thickened and bubbly. Stir in the shredded cheese. Continue heating and stirring till cheese is melted. Makes 6 servings.

Big-Meal Soup

1 pound dry green *or* yellow split peas
7 cups water
1 1-pound ham bone *or* 1 pound smoked pork
   hocks (ham hocks)
2 medium carrots, coarsely chopped (1 cup)
1 medium onion, chopped (½ cup)
1 teaspoon salt
1 16-ounce can tomatoes, cut up
1 medium green pepper, chopped (½ cup)
1 stalk celery, chopped (½ cup)

Rinse peas. In 4-quart Dutch oven combine split peas, water, ham bone or pork hocks, carrots, onion and salt. Bring to boiling. Reduce heat; cover and simmer for 45 to 60 minutes or till peas are tender. Remove ham bone and cut off meat. Discard bone.

Press *half* the pea mixture through a sieve. (Or, process in blender or food processor till smooth.) Return to Dutch oven. Stir in meat. Add *undrained* tomatoes, green pepper, and celery. Simmer 15 to 20 minutes or till celery and green pepper are done. Season to taste with salt and pepper. Makes 6 to 8 servings.

Soaking Dry Beans

Dry beans and dry whole peas need soaking before cooking, but split peas and lentils do not. Rinse and drain all the dried products before cooking.

To soak, combine dry beans with the specified amount of water in Dutch oven. Bring to boiling. Reduce heat; simmer 2 minutes. Remove from heat. Cover; let stand 1 hour. Or, soak beans in water overnight.

Curry-Vegetable Soup

Buttermilk adds a tangy flavor to this spicy bean soup—

1 pound dry baby
   lima beans (2½
   cups)
8 cups water
1 large onion,
   chopped (1 cup)
1 tablespoon instant
   chicken bouillon
   granules
• • •
2 cups cauliflowerets
   or 1 10-ounce
   package frozen
   cauliflower

2 medium apples,
   peeled and
   chopped (2 cups)
2 medium carrots,
   sliced (1 cup)
1 tablespoon curry
   powder
1½ teaspoons salt
¼ teaspoon ground
   cardamom
• • •
4 beaten egg yolks
2 cups buttermilk
Snipped parsley

Rinse beans. In a Dutch oven or kettle combine beans and the water. Bring to boiling. Reduce heat; simmer 2 minutes. Remove from heat. Cover; let stand 1 hour. (Or, soak beans in the water overnight in a covered pan.) *Do not drain.* Add onion and bouillon granules to beans. Cover and simmer 1 hour or till beans are nearly tender.

Add cauliflowerets, apples, carrots, curry, salt, and cardamom. Simmer the mixture 30 to 40 minutes more or till vegetables are tender. Combine beaten egg yolks and buttermilk; add to soup. Heat through; do not boil. Serve in soup bowls. Sprinkle with parsley. Makes 8 servings.

Pinto Bean Gumbo

1⅔ cups dry pinto
    beans *or* dry navy
    beans
  7 cups water
  1 large onion,
    chopped (1 cup)
½ cup diced salt pork
    (4 ounces)
½ teaspoon salt
  1 bay leaf
  2 cups fresh okra,
    thinly sliced
  1 16-ounce can toma-
    toes, cut up

  1 12-ounce can whole
    kernel corn,
    drained
  2 teaspoons worces-
    tershire sauce
  1 teaspoon salt
  1 teaspoon sugar
  1 teaspoon dried
    thyme, crushed
½ teaspoon bottled hot
    pepper sauce

Rinse beans. In 5-quart Dutch oven or kettle combine beans and the water. Bring to boiling. Reduce heat; cover and simmer 2 minutes. Remove from heat. Cover; let stand 1 hour. (Or, soak beans in the water overnight in a covered pan.) *Do not drain.*

Add onion, salt pork, the ½ teaspoon salt, and the bay leaf to beans and liquid. Bring to boiling. Reduce heat; cover and simmer 2 to 2½ hours or till beans are tender. Add sliced okra, *undrained* tomatoes, drained corn, worcestershire sauce, the 1 teaspoon salt, sugar, thyme, and bottled hot pepper sauce. Simmer the mixture 30 minutes or till okra is tender. Remove bay leaf before serving. Makes 10 servings.

Onion Supper Soup

3 large onions, thinly sliced
1 clove garlic, minced
¼ cup butter *or* margarine
4 cups Vegetable Stock (see recipe, page 174) *or*
    Browned Beef Stock (see recipe, page 169)
4 thick slices French bread
4 ounces Swiss *or* gruyère cheese, sliced
    Grated parmesan cheese

In covered saucepan cook onions and garlic in butter over low heat 20 minutes or till very tender; stir occasionally. Add stock and ¼ teaspoon *pepper*. Bring to boiling; cover and simmer 15 minutes. Meanwhile, toast bread. Arrange slices on baking sheet. Top each with sliced cheese; sprinkle with parmesan. Broil 2 to 3 minutes or till cheese melts. Ladle soup into 4 bowls. Top each with a toast slice. Makes 4 servings.

Bean-Bacon Chowder

6 slices bacon, cut up
1 cup chopped onion
2 tablespoons all-purpose flour
3 cups milk
2 medium potatoes, peeled
¼ teaspoon dried thyme, crushed
1 22-ounce jar baked beans
¼ cup snipped parsley

In saucepan cook bacon and onion till bacon is lightly browned and onion is tender. Blend in flour. Add milk; cook and stir till bubbly. Dice potatoes; add with thyme, 1 teaspoon *salt*, and ⅛ teaspoon *pepper*. Cover; simmer 12 to 15 minutes or till potatoes are done. Stir in beans; heat through. Top with parsley. Serves 6.

Minestrone

1½ cups dry navy beans
9 cups water
2 medium carrots,
    chopped (1 cup)
6 slices bacon
1 large onion,
    chopped (1 cup)
2 stalks celery,
    chopped (1 cup)
1 clove garlic, minced
2 16-ounce cans toma-
    toes, cut up
2 cups finely shredded
    cabbage
2 medium zucchini,
    sliced (about
    2 cups)

2 teaspoons salt
1 teaspoon dried
    basil, crushed
½ teaspoon ground
    sage
¼ teaspoon pepper
3 ounces fine noodles
    (1½ cups) *or*
    ½ recipe
    Whole Wheat
    Noodles (see
    recipe, page 177)

Rinse beans. In Dutch oven or kettle combine beans and the water. Bring to boiling; reduce heat and simmer 2 minutes. Remove from heat. Cover; let stand 1 hour. (Or, soak beans in the water overnight in a covered pan.) *Do not drain.* Add carrots. Cover and simmer 2½ to 3 hours.

Meanwhile, in a skillet cook bacon till crisp. Drain, reserving 2 tablespoons drippings. Crumble bacon; set aside. Cook onion, celery, and garlic in reserved drippings till vegetables are almost tender; drain. Add to beans along with *undrained* tomatoes, cabbage, zucchini, salt, basil, sage, and pepper. Bring to boiling; stir in noodles. Reduce heat and simmer 20 to 25 minutes more or till noodles are tender. Stir in crumbled bacon. Top each serving with grated parmesan cheese, if desired. Makes 8 servings.

Lentil-Pepperoni Soup

Serve this stick-to-the-ribs soup with bulgur wheat, also called cracked wheat—

1½ cups dry lentils
  4 ounces pepperoni, thinly sliced and halved
  1 medium onion, chopped (½ cup)
  1 6-ounce can tomato paste
1½ teaspoons salt
  ¼ teaspoon dried oregano, crushed

  ¼ teaspoon ground sage
  ⅛ teaspoon cayenne
  2 medium tomatoes, peeled and cut up
  1 medium carrot, thinly sliced (½ cup)
  1 stalk celery, sliced (½ cup)
  ½ cup bulgur wheat

Rinse lentils; in Dutch oven combine with 6 cups *water*, pepperoni, onion, tomato paste, salt, oregano, sage, and cayenne. Bring to boiling. Reduce heat; cover and simmer for 30 minutes, stirring occasionally. Add tomatoes, carrot, and celery; cover and simmer 40 minutes longer.

Meanwhile, cook bulgur according to package directions. Mound bulgur in soup. Makes 6 to 8 servings.

Crockery cooking directions: Use ingredients as listed above. Rinse lentils. In large saucepan combine 5 cups *water* and lentils; bring to boiling. Reduce heat; cover and simmer 30 minutes. *Do not drain.* In electric slow crockery cooker combine lentils and their liquid with remaining ingredients, except bulgur. Cover and cook on low-heat setting for 10 hours. Cook bulgur according to package directions. Stir soup before serving; serve as directed above.

Spicy Eggplant Parmesan Stew

2 slices bacon
1 medium eggplant, peeled and cubed (5 cups)
1 medium onion, chopped (½ cup)
1 clove garlic, minced
1½ cups beef broth (see tip, page 174)
1 8-ounce can tomato sauce

½ teaspoon dried oregano, crushed
¼ teaspoon salt
⅛ teaspoon crushed dried red pepper

• • •

6 ounces mozzarella cheese, sliced
¼ cup grated parmesan cheese (1 ounce)

In a 3-quart saucepan cook bacon till crisp. Drain, reserving bacon drippings in pan. Crumble bacon and set aside for garnish.

In the reserved bacon drippings cook the cubed eggplant, chopped onion, and minced garlic, covered, over low heat till eggplant is golden, stirring occasionally. Stir in the beef broth, tomato sauce, oregano, salt, and crushed red pepper. Bring mixture to boiling. Reduce heat; cover and simmer about 15 minutes or till the eggplant is tender.

Spoon the eggplant mixture into 4 individual casseroles. Top each casserole with sliced mozzarella cheese; sprinkle with the grated parmesan cheese. Place under broiler; broil till cheese melts. Garnish with the reserved bacon. Makes 4 servings.

Italian Bean Soup

1 cup dry navy beans
1 8-ounce can tomato sauce
1 cup chopped onion
1 cup chopped carrots
½ cup chopped green pepper
2 cloves garlic, minced
2 tablespoons instant beef bouillon granules
1½ teaspoons *each* dried basil, crushed, *and* dried oregano, crushed
½ cup macaroni

Rinse beans; add 8 cups *water*. Boil 2 minutes. Remove from heat; cover and let stand 1 hour. (Or, soak in the water overnight.) *Do not drain.* Stir in 1 teaspoon *salt* and remaining ingredients, except macaroni. Cover, simmer 1½ hours. Stir in macaroni; cook, uncovered, 10 to 15 minutes. Makes 6 to 8 servings.

Mexican Red Bean and Pineapple Soup

1 cup chopped onion
½ cup chopped green pepper
1 clove garlic, minced
1 tablespoon cooking oil
2 16-ounce cans red kidney beans
1 16-ounce can tomatoes, cut up
½ cup diced fully cooked ham
1 bay leaf
¼ teaspoon *each* ground cumin, ground cinnamon, *and* dried oregano, crushed
1 8¼-ounce can crushed pineapple

Cook onion, green pepper, and garlic in oil till vegetables are tender. Stir in 1 teaspoon *salt* and remaining ingredients, except pineapple. Cover; simmer 30 minutes. Stir in *undrained* pineapple; heat through. Serves 4 to 6.

QUICK SOUPS

Butter Bean Soup

½ pound bulk pork sausage
¼ cup sliced green onion
3 16-ounce cans butter beans
2 cups milk
1 10¾-ounce can condensed tomato soup
1 teaspoon salt
½ teaspoon dried thyme, crushed
Dash pepper

In large saucepan cook sausage and onion till sausage is done. Drain off fat. To sausage add *undrained* beans, milk, soup, salt, thyme, and pepper. Heat to boiling. Reduce heat; cover and simmer 10 minutes. Top with more sliced green onions, if desired. Serves 6.

Cheese-Bean Chowder

- 2 12-ounce cans whole kernel corn with sweet peppers
- 1 16-ounce can red kidney beans, drained
- 1½ cups milk
- ¾ teaspoon chili powder
- ½ teaspoon salt
- 1 6-ounce roll cheese food with hickory smoke flavor, cut up

In 3-quart saucepan combine *undrained* corn, the beans, milk, chili powder, and salt. Cook, stirring occasionally, over medium-low heat till just bubbly. Add cheese; heat and stir till cheese melts and soup is hot. Serves 4.

Black-Eyed Pea and Rice Stew

Patterned after the Southern favorite "Hopping John," this stew is delicious served with corn bread—

2 15-ounce cans black-eyed peas	½ teaspoon garlic salt
3 cups water	¼ teaspoon pepper
1 large onion, sliced	¼ teaspoon bottled hot pepper sauce
2 stalks celery, sliced (1 cup)	½ cup long grain rice
2 slices bacon, diced	
1 teaspoon instant chicken bouillon granules	

In a large saucepan stir together the *undrained* black-eyed peas, the water, sliced onion, sliced celery, diced bacon, chicken bouillon granules, garlic salt, pepper, and bottled hot pepper sauce. Bring mixture to boiling. Stir in the uncooked rice. Reduce heat; cover and simmer for 20 to 25 minutes or till the rice is done. Makes 4 servings.

Egg-Corn Chowder

4 hard-cooked eggs
1 17-ounce can cream-style corn
2 cups milk
1 green pepper, finely chopped (½ cup)
1 tablespoon minced dried onion
1 tablespoon prepared mustard
¾ teaspoon salt

Remove yolks from *two* eggs; set aside. Chop remaining eggs and whites. In saucepan combine chopped eggs with remaining ingredients. Cover, simmer 15 minutes. Sieve reserved yolks atop. Serves 4.

Cabbage-Cheese Soup

3½ cups milk
1 10¾-ounce can condensed cream of potato soup
2 cups coarsely chopped cabbage
1 medium carrot, coarsely shredded (½ cup)
1 cup shredded process Swiss cheese (4 ounces)
½ teaspoon caraway seed
¼ teaspoon pepper

In saucepan stir milk .into soup. Cook and stir till bubbly; stir in cabbage and carrot. Cover and simmer 5 minutes or till cabbage is done. Stir in cheese, caraway, and pepper. Heat and stir till cheese melts. Makes 4 servings.

SOUP-MAKING BASICS

Stocks — Noodles — Dumplings — Croutons and Crackers

Here's everything you need to know to make soups and stews from scratch, including shortcuts to home-style flavor.

A good stock is the basis of a great soup. You can make one by simmering meat bones, vegetables, and seasonings in a stockpot. You'll find recipes for beef, chicken, veal, vegetable, and fish stocks, as well as one that uses vegetable leftovers and your choice of meat bones.

Crown your soup with your choice of noodles, dumplings, or croutons. Or, serve with crackers you make yourself.

STOCKS

Beef Stock

Try making Browned Beef Stock when you want a stock with a richer, browned flavor—

6 pounds beef soup bones (neck bones, arm bones, shank bones, *or* marrow bones)
1 large onion, sliced
2 carrots, cut up
2 stalks celery with leaves, cut up

1 large tomato, cut up (optional)
8 whole black peppercorns
4 sprigs parsley
1 bay leaf
1 clove garlic, halved
1 tablespoon salt
12 cups cold water

In a large stockpot or Dutch oven place beef soup bones; onion; carrots; celery; tomato, if desired; peppercorns; parsley; bay leaf; garlic; and salt. Add the water. Bring to boiling. Reduce heat; cover and simmer for 4 to 5 hours.

Lift out beef bones with a slotted spoon. Strain the stock through a sieve lined with 1 or 2 layers of cheesecloth; discard the seasonings. Clarify stock, if desired (see tip, page 170).

Skim off the fat with a metal spoon, or chill the stock and lift off the solidified fat. Makes about 10 cups stock.

Browned Beef Stock: Use ingredients as listed above. Spread beef bones, onion slices, and carrots in a large shallow roasting pan so that the beef bones will brown evenly. Bake the bones in a 450° oven about 30 minutes or till the bones are well browned, turning occasionally with tongs. Drain off any fat.

In a large stockpot or Dutch oven place the browned bones, onion, and carrots. Add the celery; tomato, if desired; peppercorns; parsley; bay leaf; garlic; and salt. Add the water. Bring to boiling. Reduce heat; cover and simmer for 4 to 5 hours.

Strain, clarify, and remove fat as directed above.

Clarifying

Clarify beef stock, chicken stock, or white stock when you want a clear soup. Clarifying removes solid flecks that are too small to be strained out with cheesecloth, but which will muddy a soup's appearance.

To clarify, stir together ¼ cup cold water, 1 egg white, and 1 egg shell, crushed. Add to strained stock; bring to boiling. Remove from heat and let stand 5 minutes. Strain again through a sieve lined with cheesecloth.

Stock Making

• It's not necessary to peel or trim vegetables for stocks, since they will be strained out. Just wash and cut them up.

• Start with cold water to extract the most flavor from meat and vegetables.

• Simmer stocks slowly for best flavor—bubbles should form slowly and burst before reaching the surface.

• To avoid spills, ladle stock into the strainer rather than pouring it.

• Avoid over-seasoning stocks for other recipes.

Basic Stock

Use strong-flavored vegetables with the beef or ham bones; more delicate ones with chicken pieces—

4 pounds meaty beef bones *or* 2½ pounds chicken necks, wings, and backs *or* 2 pounds meaty ham bones
3 medium onions, quartered
1½ cups celery leaves
6 sprigs parsley
4 whole black peppercorns

2 *or* 3 bay leaves
1 *or* 2 cloves garlic, halved
1 tablespoon salt*
1 tablespoon dried basil, crushed *or* 2 teaspoons dried thyme, crushed
10 cups cold water

Choose 2 or 3 of the following:

1½ cups potato peelings
1½ cups carrot peelings
1½ cups turnip leaves *or* peelings
1½ cups parsnip leaves *or* peelings

4 *or* 5 outer cabbage leaves
¾ cup sliced green onion tops
¾ cup sliced leek tops

In a 10-quart stockpot or Dutch oven place the beef bones, chicken pieces, or ham bones. Add the quartered onions, celery leaves, parsley, whole peppercorns, bay leaves, garlic, salt, and basil or thyme. Add the cold water. Choose 2 or 3 of the vegetable peelings, leaves, or tops. Add these to the stockpot or Dutch oven.

Bring mixture to boiling. Reduce heat; cover and simmer over low heat for about 3 hours. Lift out the meat bones with a slotted spoon; set aside.

Strain the stock by ladling it through a sieve lined

*Reduce salt to 1 teaspoon when using ham bones, then season finished stock to taste.

with 1 or 2 layers of cheesecloth; discard vegetables and seasonings. Clarify the stock, if desired (see tip on page 170). Skim off the excess fat with a metal spoon, or chill the stock and lift off the solidified fat.

When bones are cool enough to handle, remove meat from bones; reserve meat for another use, if desired. Discard bones. Store the stock and any leftover meat in separate covered containers in the refrigerator or freezer. Makes 7 to 8 cups stock.

Storing Stock

Ladle the finished stock into pint or quart jars or other non-plastic containers while it is still hot. Cover and refrigerate to chill quickly. If you are saving the meat for another use, store it in a separate container from the stock for easy use.

Stock may be stored in the refrigerator for a few days, or in the freezer for up to 6 months. Be sure to label the contents of each container with the type of stock, quantity, and the date.

If you frequently use stock in small quantities, freeze it in ice cube trays. When frozen, place frozen stock cubes in a plastic bag and return them to the freezer. Measure the volume of a melted cube to determine the exact amount of stock in each cube (approximately 2 tablespoons).

Chicken Stock

    2 pounds bony chicken pieces (backs, necks, and
        wings)
    3 stalks celery with leaves, cut up
    2 medium carrots, cut up
 1½ teaspoons salt
    ¼ teaspoon pepper
    6 cups water
    1 large onion, cut into thirds
    3 whole cloves

In a 5-quart stockpot or Dutch oven combine chicken
pieces, celery, carrots, salt, and pepper; add water.
Stud each onion third with a whole clove. Add to pot.
Bring to boiling. Reduce heat; cover and simmer about
1 hour or till chicken is tender.

Lift out chicken pieces with a slotted spoon. Strain
stock through a sieve lined with 1 or 2 layers of cheesecloth; discard vegetables.

Clarify stock, if desired (see tip on page 170). Skim
off fat with a metal spoon, or chill stock and lift off the
solidified fat.

When chicken is cool enough to handle, remove
chicken from bones and save meat for another use, if
desired. Makes 5 cups stock.

Crockery cooking directions: Use ingredients as
listed above *except* decrease water to *4 cups.*

In an electric slow crockery cooker place chicken,
celery, carrots, salt, and pepper. Add 4 cups water.
Stud each onion third with a whole clove; add to
cooker. Cover and cook on low-heat setting for 8 to
10 hours. Remove chicken and vegetables from crockery cooker with a slotted spoon. Strain and clarify
stock; remove fat as directed above. Makes about 4½
cups stock.

Stock Substitutions

When a recipe calls for beef or chicken broth, use one of the stock recipes in this chapter. Or, if you're in a hurry, you don't need to start from scratch. Excellent commercial substitutes are available. And, if you don't have the specified flavor, substitute a different one—you may even prefer it!

Canned beef and chicken broths are ready to use straight from the can. Canned condensed beef and chicken broths are also available. These must be diluted according to can directions.

Instant bouillon granules and cubes can be purchased in beef, chicken, vegetable, and onion flavors. These should be mixed with water according to package directions before using as a broth substitute.

Vegetable Stock

2 tablespoons butter *or* margarine	½ teaspoon dried thyme, crushed
3 carrots, chopped	2 tomatoes, cut up
2 stalks celery with leaves, chopped	1 cup shredded lettuce
1 large onion, chopped	2 sprigs parsley
1 turnip, chopped	1½ teaspoons salt
1 clove garlic, halved	¼ teaspoon pepper

In large saucepan melt butter. Add carrots, celery, onion, turnip, garlic, and thyme. Cover and cook over low heat 30 minutes or till vegetables are tender, stirring occasionally. Add remaining ingredients and 6 cups cold *water*. Bring to boiling. Reduce heat; cover and simmer 2 hours. Strain; discard vegetables. Makes 4½ cups.

Fish Stock

1½ pounds fresh *or* frozen dressed fish (with head
    and tail)
1 small onion, chopped
1 stalk celery with leaves, chopped
3 sprigs parsley
½ lemon, sliced
1 teaspoon salt
3 whole black peppercorns
3 whole cloves

Cut up fish, if necessary, to fit in a large saucepan.
Add the onion, celery, parsley, lemon, salt, peppercorns and cloves. Add 6 cups cold *water*. Bring to boiling. Reduce heat; cover and simmer 30 minutes. Strain
through sieve lined with 1 or 2 layers of cheesecloth.
Reserve fish for another use; discard skin, bones, and
seasonings. Makes 4 cups.

White Stock

4 pounds veal
    knuckle, cut up
2 stalks celery with
    leaves, cut up
2 medium carrots,
    cut up
1 tablespoon salt
1 large onion,
    quartered

4 whole cloves
2 sprigs parsley
1 clove garlic, halved
1 small bay leaf
1 teaspoon dried
    thyme, crushed

In stockpot or Dutch oven place veal, celery, carrots,
and salt. Stud each onion quarter with a clove; add
to pot. To make a *bouquet garni*, place parsley, garlic,
bay leaf, and thyme on an 8-inch square of cheesecloth. Bring up edges and tie with thread; add to pot.
Add 10 cups cold *water*. Cover and simmer 5 hours.
Remove *bouquet garni* and veal; discard. Strain stock;

clarify, if desired (see tip on page 170). Skim fat, or chill and lift off fat. Makes 9½ cups stock.

Crockery cooking directions: Use ingredients as listed above, *except* use only 2½ to 3 pounds veal knuckle. In slow electric crockery cooker place 2½ to 3 pounds veal knuckle, celery, carrots, and salt. Stud each onion quarter with a clove; add to cooker. Make *bouquet garni* as above; add to cooker. Add 6 to 6½ cups *water*. Cover; cook on low-heat setting 12 to 15 hours. Strain, clarify, and remove fat. Makes 6 cups.

NOODLES

Homemade Noodles

Use these in any recipe that calls for noodles. Or, substitute packaged or frozen noodles, following the cooking directions on the package—

1 beaten egg
2 tablespoons milk
½ teaspoon salt
1 cup all-purpose flour

In mixing bowl combine egg, milk, and salt. Stir in enough of the flour to make a stiff dough. Cover and let rest for 10 minutes.

On floured surface roll dough to a 16x12-inch rectangle. Let stand 20 minutes. Roll up loosely; cut into ¼-inch slices. Unroll; cut into desired lengths. Spread out and let dry on rack 2 hours. Store in airtight container till ready to use.

Cook noodles as directed in recipe, or drop into a large amount of boiling salted water or soup. Cook, uncovered, 10 to 12 minutes. Makes about 3 cups.

Whole Wheat Noodles: Prepare as directed above, *except* substitute ½ cup *whole wheat flour* for ½ cup of the all-purpose flour.

Puffy Cheese Noodles

    1 beaten egg
    1 tablespoon milk
    ¾ cup all-purpose flour
    ¼ cup grated parmesan cheese
    1 teaspoon baking powder

Mix together egg and milk. In a mixing bowl stir together flour, parmesan, baking powder, and ¼ teaspoon *salt*. Stir in egg mixture to make a stiff dough.

Turn dough onto a lightly floured surface. Roll out to a 12x12-inch square. Roll up jelly roll–style; slice into ¼-inch-wide strips. Unroll. Cut into desired lengths. Use as directed in recipe, or spread out and let dry on a rack up to 2 hours. Drop noodles into boiling salted water or prepared soup. Cook, uncovered, for 10 to 12 minutes. Makes about 2½ cups.

Green Noodles

    1¼ cups torn spinach leaves
    2 tablespoons water
    1 egg
    ½ teaspoon salt
    1¼ cups all-purpose flour

In saucepan combine spinach and water. Cover and cook till spinach is very tender. Cool slightly; place spinach and liquid in blender container. Add egg and salt; cover and blend till smooth. Transfer to bowl. Add enough of the flour to make a stiff dough. Knead on lightly floured surface 1 minute. Roll very thin on floured surface. Let rest 20 minutes. Roll up loosely. Slice ¼ inch wide. Unroll. Cut into desired lengths. Spread out; let dry on a rack for 2 hours. Store in airtight container till needed. Use as directed in recipe, or cook, uncovered, in boiling salted water or prepared soup for 10 to 12 minutes or till tender. Makes about 3½ cups.

DUMPLINGS

Danish Dumplings

These are made like cream puffs—

- ½ cup water
- ¼ cup butter *or* margarine
- ½ cup all-purpose flour
- 1 teaspoon baking powder
- ⅛ teaspoon salt
- 2 eggs
- 1 tablespoon snipped parsley

In a saucepan combine the water and the butter or margarine; bring to boiling. Add the flour, baking powder, and salt all at once, stirring vigorously. Cook, stirring constantly, till mixture forms a ball that doesn't separate. Remove from heat; cool slightly. Add the eggs, one at a time, beating well after each addition till mixture is smooth. Stir in the parsley.

Drop dumpling dough from a tablespoon to make 12 mounds atop bubbling soup or stew. Cover and simmer for 20 minutes (do not lift cover). Makes 12 dumplings.

Fluffy Dumplings

To keep dough from sticking to spoon, dip spoon into the hot soup or stew liquid before forming each dumpling—

- 1 cup all-purpose flour
- 2 teaspoons baking powder
- ½ teaspoon salt
- ½ cup milk
- 2 tablespoons cooking oil *or* melted shortening

In a mixing bowl thoroughly stir together the flour, baking powder, and salt. Combine the milk and the cooking oil or melted shortening; add liquid mixture all at once to the dry ingredients, stirring just till moistened.

Drop the dumpling dough from a tablespoon to make 4 to 6 mounds atop bubbling soup or stew. Cover tightly and simmer for 15 minutes (do not lift cover). Makes 4 to 6 dumplings.

Easy Dumplings

Here's an easy way to mix up delicious dumplings—

> 2 cups packaged biscuit mix
> ⅔ cup milk

In mixing bowl place biscuit mix. Add milk all at once; stir just till mixture is moistened.

Drop dough from a tablespoon to make 10 to 12 mounds atop the bubbling soup or stew. Simmer dumplings, uncovered, about 10 minutes. Cover and simmer 10 minutes longer (do not lift cover). Makes 10 to 12 dumplings.

Lemon Dumplings

> 1 cup all-purpose flour
> 1½ teaspoons baking powder
> ½ teaspoon salt
> 1 beaten egg
> ½ cup milk
> 1 tablespoon snipped parsley
> ½ teaspoon finely shredded lemon peel
> 1 teaspoon lemon juice

Stir together flour, baking powder, and salt. Combine remaining ingredients. Add milk mixture to dry ingredients; stir just till moistened. Drop dough from tablespoon to make 6 mounds atop bubbling soup or stew. Cover; simmer 20 minutes (do not lift cover). Makes 6.

Matzo Balls

    2 eggs
    ½ cup matzo meal
    ¼ cup club soda
    2 tablespoons rendered chicken fat, melted
    ½ teaspoon salt

Beat eggs well; stir in matzo meal, club soda, chicken fat, salt, and dash *pepper*. Mix till smooth. Cover and chill at least 2 hours. Drop dough from a tablespoon to make 8 mounds atop bubbling soup or stew. Cover and simmer 30 minutes (do not lift cover). Makes 8.

Corn Dumplings

    1 cup water
    ⅓ cup yellow cornmeal
    ½ teaspoon salt
       Dash pepper
    1 beaten egg
    ⅔ cup all-purpose flour
    1 teaspoon baking powder
    1 12-ounce can whole kernel corn with sweet
       peppers, drained

In medium saucepan combine water, cornmeal, salt, and pepper. Cook and stir till thickened and bubbly. Remove from heat; cool slightly. Add egg, beating till smooth. Stir together flour and baking powder. Add to cornmeal mixture; beat well. Stir in the drained corn.

Drop dough from a tablespoon to make 12 mounds atop bubbling soup or stew. Cover and simmer for 10 to 12 minutes (do not lift cover). Makes 12.

Herb Dumplings

These dumplings are doubly special, flavored with herb and sour cream—

1½ cups all-purpose flour
1 tablespoon baking powder
¾ teaspoon salt
¼ teaspoon dried thyme, crushed, *or* dried sage, crushed
¾ cup dairy sour cream
¾ cup milk
2 tablespoons cooking oil *or* melted shortening

In a medium mixing bowl thoroughly stir together the flour, baking powder, salt, and dried thyme or sage. In another bowl combine the dairy sour cream, the milk, and the cooking oil or melted shortening. Add the sour cream mixture all at once to the dry ingredients in mixing bowl; stir just till all dry ingredients are thoroughly moistened.

Drop the dumpling dough from a tablespoon to make 8 mounds atop the bubbling soup or stew. Reduce the heat; cover and simmer the dumplings for about 15 minutes (do not lift cover). Makes 8 dumplings.

CRACKERS

Crackers

These homemade crackers are very much like crisp biscuits, and taste wonderful with any soup—

1 cup all-purpose flour
1 teaspoon baking powder
¼ teaspoon salt
¼ cup butter *or* margarine
¼ cup milk

Thoroughly stir together the flour, baking powder, and salt. Cut in the butter or margarine till the mixture resembles coarse crumbs. Add the milk all at once; stir till the mixture forms a ball.

Turn dough out onto a lightly floured surface. Knead dough gently 8 to 10 strokes. Roll out the dough to ¼-inch thickness. Dip a 2½-inch biscuit cutter in some flour; cut straight down through dough.

Place dough rounds on a greased baking sheet. Bake in a 400° oven for 10 minutes. Split the hot crackers with a sharp knife; spread out, cut sides up, on the same baking sheet. Return crackers to the oven and bake 4 to 6 minutes longer or till crackers are golden brown. Makes about 24 crackers.

Whole Wheat Crackers

Serve these special crackers with your favorite vegetable soup—

    1 cup whole wheat flour
    1 cup all-purpose flour
    ⅓ cup sugar
    2 teaspoons baking powder
    1 teaspoon baking soda
    ½ teaspoon salt
    ½ teaspoon cream of tartar
    ½ cup butter *or* margarine
    ¾ cup buttermilk

In a mixing bowl stir together the whole wheat flour, all-purpose flour, sugar, baking powder, soda, salt, and cream of tartar. Cut in the butter or margarine till mixture resembles coarse crumbs. Add buttermilk all at once. Stir with a fork just till dough follows fork around bowl.

On floured surface roll out dough to 1/16-inch thickness. Cut with a floured 2½-inch biscuit cutter; prick crackers with a fork. Place on an ungreased baking sheet. Bake in a 350° oven for 12 to 15 minutes or till lightly browned. Makes about 60.

CROUTONS

Croutons

Use white, whole wheat, rye, or any other yeast bread—

Cut bread into ½-inch cubes. Spread in a shallow baking pan. Bake in 300° oven for 30 minutes or till dry and golden. (Each slice of bread makes about ¾ cup.)

Microwave cooking directions: Spread 4 cups bread cubes in shallow baking dish. Cook, uncovered, in a countertop microwave oven on high power for 6 minutes; stir every 2 minutes.

Garlic Croutons

    4 slices bread
    3 tablespoons butter, melted
    ⅛ teaspoon garlic powder

Cut bread into ½-inch cubes. Spread in a shallow baking pan. Combine butter and garlic powder; drizzle over bread cubes. Toss to coat. Bake in 300° oven for 30 minutes. Store, covered, in the refrigerator. Makes about 2½ cups.

INDEX

A–B

189

G–O

P–R

tips